How to have a
happy
cat

How to have a
happy
cat

Andrea McHugh

hamlyn

An Hachette Livre UK Company

First published in Great Britain in 2007 by
Hamlyn, a division of Octopus Publishing Group Ltd
2–4 Heron Quays, London E14 4JP
www.octopusbooks.co.uk

Distributed in the United States and Canada by
Sterling Publishing Co., Inc.
387 Park Avenue South, New York, NY 10016-8810

ISBN 978-0-600-61658-0

A CIP catalogue record for this book is available
from the British Library
Colour Reproduction by Dot Gradations Ltd, UK
Printed and bound in Italy

10 9 8 7 6 5 4 3 2 1

The advice given in this book should not be used
as a substitute for that of a veterinary surgeon.

No cats or kittens were harmed in the making of
this book.

Unless the information given in this book is
specifically for female cats, cats are referred to
throughout as 'he'. The information is equally
applicable to both male and female cats,
unless otherwise specified.

Contents

Introduction

Cats have now officially overtaken all other pets as the most popular companion animal of the 21st century. Millions of people all over the world choose to share their lives with one or more cats, and none of us would do that if owning a cat didn't enhance our lives in many ways, making us happier people. But while our cats undoubtedly make us happy, with their unconditional love, cute personalities and apparently laid-back view of life, are we doing everything we can to ensure that our cats are as happy as they can possibly be?

Cats can sometimes be perceived as complicated or slightly mysterious creatures, but in reality their basic needs for food, water and shelter are quite simple. Yet there is so much more you can do that goes beyond this and enables you to tap into a cat's physical and emotional being, so that you will quickly have him purring in blissful contentment. Fortunately, the happier you make your cat, the better the relationship between you and the happier you become too! As you will discover while reading this book, it really is worth taking those extra steps to ensure your cat is as contented as he can be.

Most of the suggestions in this book cost very little financially: taking time to learn why your cat behaves the way he does, how he tries to communicate with you and, most importantly, what he *really* needs (rather than what we humans *assume* he needs) are the key items on your cat's happiness wish list. Vets, scientists, nutritionists and feline behaviourists are all working hard to prolong the lifespan of cats, prevent health problems and ensure that you are armed with the knowledge to provide as natural a life as possible for your cat, often in somewhat unnatural conditions, such as when he has to be kept permanently indoors. The book includes some fascinating research material, plus many tips that will have an enormous impact on your cat's physical and mental wellbeing.

So, let's get started – your cat deserves to be happy, and you deserve a happy cat! Happy reading…

1 Talking 'cat'

In the animal world, cats are considered to be experts at communicating their feelings. They certainly waste no time in informing their owners, in fairly forthright terms, whether or not they are happy!

However, if you don't understand cat speak it's easy to misinterpret some of the subtleties of their language. To have a happier cat, you need to learn more about what he's saying to you.

Subtle, and not so subtle

Our feline friends have a myriad of excellent methods of communication at their disposal including their voice, the position and size of their eyes, ears, tail and body, how the hairs on their coat lie – and, of course, some other less subtle devices, such as whether or not they choose to use their claws on you or the furniture!

What's he saying?

Because cats are so clever, even people with little experience of felines can make an educated guess as to whether one is happy or not, simply by observing his body language. However, taking time to learn more about the nuances of how cats communicate with us and with each other will greatly enhance your relationship with your pet.

Unhappy cat speak

Cats are renowned for their independence and, unlike many other animals, will not usually accept situations that make them unhappy or cause them stress. This unhappiness can manifest in many different ways, from a refusal to eat or interact to something the owner finds annoying, such as biting or urinating in strange places and hiding away in different rooms of the house. In severe cases, a loving owner can be distraught to find that their cat has actually left home and gone to live with a neighbour!

Rather than waiting until your cat has disappeared from your life for ever – through the cat flap you lovingly installed – before asking yourself 'Where did I go wrong?', it makes sense to find out how your cat tries to make you understand his state of mind.

Feline body language

Take a look at your cat. Does he feel happy? Anxious? Threatened? The truth is that he may display any or all of these emotions during a single day.

Here's how cats use a clever combination of body language techniques to convey their mood.

Eyes

It's said that the eyes are the window on the soul, and this is never more true than with the expressive eyes of a cat.

If he is feeling happy and relaxed, your cat's eyes will be half-closed, indicating that he is confident and trusting. On the other hand, if he is very anxious or curious his eyes will open wide and the pupils will expand, so that he can see better and assess the overall situation (see pages 14–15). Dilated pupils can also be an indication of agitation or excitement.

A cat is at his most vulnerable and submissive when he is sleeping and his eyes are fully closed.

Ears

If your cat is feeling happy and relaxed, his ears will be pointing forwards and slightly outwards and may move gently as he listens for any interesting sounds. If he becomes tense, his ears will be positioned slightly backwards and twitching as he tries to interpret what a particular noise means.

When a cat feels frightened, he will hold his ears up and back for protection. If this progresses to him being threatened by a dominant cat, he will flatten his ears against his skull to avoid injury to them.

Whiskers

An unhappy, frightened cat will pull his whiskers back tightly against his face, in order to make himself look smaller and therefore less threatening to another hostile cat or animal. Angry cats will push their whiskers forwards, to indicate they mean business.

If your cat is happy and relaxed, his whiskers will droop naturally to the sides.

Tail

A happy cat will probably lie down with his tail tucked under him.

A cat that is feeling very uncertain or threatened will arch his tail: a sure warning of imminent attack. However, when a cat play fights with a feline friend his tail may bristle and be held up in excitement rather than fear.

A submissive cat that is being attacked may lie down on his side and thrash his tail from side to side, to try to deter his opponent by imitating a scary snake! Alternatively, he may wrap his tail tightly around his body in an attempt to prevent possible injury.

RESEARCH

Cats have 32 muscles that control the outer ear (compared to six in the human ear). This enables them to rotate the ears independently through 180 degrees, and turn in the direction of a sound ten times more quickly than a dog.

In addition, cats have very sensitive pads on the soles of their feet and extremely fine whiskers on their forelegs, which means they are probably able to 'hear' and assess a situation quite a lot through their feet too.

Claws

A contented cat will keep his claws sheathed. In contrast, a frightened cat will unsheath those sharp talons, ready to use if necessary. However, unsheathed claws are not always a sign of aggression: for example, the cat may be curious about something and use his claws to touch and investigate an object.

Happy cat speak

Do you understand what your cat is trying to say to you? He's making a big effort to let you know what he wants and how he is feeling. All those different sounds he makes mean something, and the more successfully he communicates with you the happier he will be.

RESEARCH
Surveys show that some breeds, such as the Russian Blue, are consistently quieter and much less likely to vocalize their needs than others, although there will always be exceptions to any rule. Oriental types, such as the Siamese, can be very loud and chatty with their owners. Cats are thought to have at least 16 distinct vocal signals in their repertoire and research is still being undertaken to try to interpret exactly what they mean.

Cats mainly communicate in three ways: vocally, through body language (see pages 10–11) and through the use of smells (see pages 18–19). Cats in close contact with each other can also communicate through mutual grooming, which helps to improve the bond between them.

Purring

Purring is produced with the cat's mouth closed and fascinates researchers, who are still not certain exactly how it is done. Kittens purr when being nursed by their mothers, but it is also heard during play with siblings and social interactions with their owners.

Although most people associate purring with contentment, in some situations a frightened or injured cat may also purr, although other body language signs should help to indicate his ambivalent state of mind (see pages 10–11), so that you can respond appropriately.

Hissing and spitting

The sounds made by a defensive or aggressive cat include hissing, spitting, growling and snarling. They are produced when the cat holds his mouth in a fixed, open position. Displaying the teeth, hissing and spitting are not observed in play fighting.

Cats become very adept at training their owner

Miaow

A cat miaows with his mouth open and then gradually closing – similar to the way we speak. Another example of this type of communication is when a male or female is calling to attract a mate.

Miaowing is usually a friendly interaction, and some cats develop distinctly different miaows for different situations: perhaps a short 'chirrup', a trilling sound or a prolonged miaow to let you know they want to be fed or would like to go out. Cats will perform a low, throaty miaow when they feel threatened.

Quiet, please

Some cats become very adept at training their owners, particularly if they receive immediate attention every time they open their mouths. Unfortunately, persistent, inappropriate 'talking' can be a sign of attention-seeking behaviour, which may become tiresome and annoying. In addition, an owner who constantly gives in to a cat's vocal demands for food can end up with an obese, unhappy cat.

To avoid falling into the trap of being completely manipulated by your cat, try to get into the habit of waiting for a moment of silence before you respond to any of his demands.

Happy to see you...

Cats are predatory animals by nature and are always happy when hunting, even if it is only in play. A cat's eyes are cleverly designed to help them hunt as efficiently as possible. By learning how your cat sees the world and how this affects his behaviour, you can begin to look at things through his eyes and make your relationship with him even happier.

Happy cat tip

Happily, cats are not particularly prone to the same hereditary eye problems as dogs and humans, and blindness is relatively rare unless caused by injury or disease. However, some breeds – such as the Persian – may experience more difficulties, and daily wiping of the delicate eye area will help to keep it clean (see pages 90—91).

A cat's eyes are situated on the front of his skull and are relatively large compared to the size of the rest of his body. This arrangement provides him with excellent binocular vision, and allows him to judge distances accurately when stalking and hunting.

Pupils

Unlike in most mammals, the pupils of a cat's eye are slit-like rather than circular in shape. Depending on the available light, they will expand or contract in order to let more light in or protect the retina at the back of the eye. A cat's eyes can appear huge at times, as the pupils are capable of expanding by up to three times more than in the human eye.

Going wild

Cats are very clever at catching mice and other wildlife, which some owners find distressing – almost as if there is another side to their home-loving pet that wouldn't usually hurt a fly. Remember, though, that a cat is merely satisfying his natural instincts and is not doing this out of malice. He will be very unhappy and confused if you suddenly start shouting at him when he proudly brings home a 'present' for you.

Cats are very well suited visually to stalking and capturing prey in half-light, such as at dawn and dusk. If your cat has access to the great outdoors, you can help to protect birds and other wildlife by keeping him inside at these times, when such creatures are most vulnerable.

RESEARCH

Have you ever wondered why your cat's eyes appear to glow in the dark if they are caught in the headlights of a car? This is caused by the tapetum, which consists of reflective pigments located at the back of the eye. Unabsorbed light passes through the retina and bounces back from this reflective layer, so the retina can detect it. The tapetum increases the efficiency of the cat's eyes in low light by up to 40 per cent.

Colour vision

The structure of cats' eyes means they have very poor colour vision. This is because they are night hunters (cats are eight times better at seeing in the dark than we are) and the light-detecting cells in the retina consist mainly of those that detect monochromes – black and white. However, the closer a cat gets to an object the better he is able to make out its colour, although his eyes differentiate fewer colours than ours, with reds tending to merge into shades of grey and black.

Creatures of habit

It can be very irritating if your cat wakes you each morning at 4am with a demand for food and fun, or is still happily climbing the walls at midnight when the rest of the family is trying to sleep. To live harmoniously with your cat, it is important that he learns to adapt to your routine, rather than the other way round.

Cats are meat eaters that consume calorie-rich protein, so (unlike herbivores) they do not need to eat continually. They restore their energy through the healing powers of sleep and domestic cats can happily snooze undisturbed for anything from 12 to 20 hours a day.

Cats are at their most active at dawn and dusk, when they are biologically programmed to hunt prey. You may notice that this is when your cat has a 'mad half hour' and is apparently overwhelmed with excess energy, racing around, playing, leaping and generally entertaining you before he flops back down to have another nap!

Let sleeping cats lie

Owners often spend a small fortune on buying their cat a designer bed and then wonder why he turns up his nose at it. Cats are renowned for choosing their own beds, and your pet may return to the same place for a few weeks before abandoning it, for no apparent reason, in favour of somewhere else – perhaps even the basket you bought him months ago!

To keep your cat happy, don't try to force him to sleep somewhere he doesn't want to. Provide him with choices: you may find that at times he prefers to sleep in an elevated position, perhaps on top of

Cats are at their most active at dawn and dusk

a cupboard, where he can safely observe the house and determine that no feline intruders are likely to bother him. This is particularly important in multi-cat households, where disputes can arise without you necessarily being aware of them.

If your cat is naturally timid he may prefer to sleep somewhere he feels really secure, such as behind the sofa. However, if he suddenly appears to be hiding away then you may have to turn detective and discover if he is feeling particularly threatened by something, such as a neighbouring cat sneaking in through his cat flap.

Happy cat tip

Observing when and how often your cat sleeps will help you to notice any changes that may indicate physical or emotional problems. Remember that older cats naturally tend to sleep more than younger cats. Providing thick, thermal, heat-reflective bedding will help your pet to maintain a comfortable body temperature, whatever his age.

Do not disturb

Keep your cat happy by allowing him to sleep for as long as he wants. Encourage any children in the family not to disturb him when he's having a nap, even if he looks particularly cute! A cat that is woken abruptly may fear he is under attack and use his teeth or claws to defend himself.

Wild at heart

Finding out more about how cats naturally live in the wild, and how much these felines have in common with today's domestic cats, can help you to understand your own cat's behaviour.

The more you understand about how your cat thinks and feels, the more likely you are to provide him with the perfect home and a fulfilling and happy life.

Grooming

Both wild and domestic cats are naturally very clean creatures – some might say obsessed with making themselves look like Kings of the Jungle. But there's more to grooming than this.

Wild cats will clean off all blood to avoid attracting the attention of any other predators. In addition, the weaker the scent a cat gives off, the more difficult it will be for his prey to smell him, so hunting becomes much more efficient.

Some cats, particularly longhaired ones such as Persians, get very distressed if their coats become dirty and matted and they are unable to clean themselves properly.

Basic instincts

Wild cats have to hunt for food in order to survive. They do this by stalking their unsuspecting prey at a safe distance, creeping towards it and then pouncing. They then kill it with a decisive bite from their long, sharp teeth.

It is thought that humans domesticated cats about 3,500 years ago to catch rodents and protect precious grain, and even though many domestic cats no longer have to do this because their human owners feed them, they still maintain a strong hunting instinct. You can keep your cat happy by providing him with plenty of toys and games that allow him to stalk, creep and pounce so that his hunting instinct is satisfied (see pages 114–115).

RESEARCH
Today there are over 35 breeds of wild cat and about 300 breeds of domestic cat. The largest of all cats is the African lion. It is estimated that approximately 100,000 tigers once roamed the earth, but today the number has fallen to about 5,000. Cheetahs are the fastest mammals on earth, running at 100 kmph (63 mph), although they only run for short distances (around 500 m/⅓ mile), to avoid overheating.

Feed me

Both wild and domestic cats are carnivores, which means they are predators and eat the flesh of the animals they kill. You will not make your cat happy by putting him on a vegetarian diet, as the lack of protein and necessary nutrients will make him extremely ill.

Territory

Most wild cats are loners that fend for themselves in adult life. They spend a lot of time watching out for passing prey or other predators that might enter their hunting range, and the rest sleeping to conserve energy. Cats need to know their territory well, and mark it with faeces, urine or pheromones (glandular secretions) from their paws.

Domestic cats are also very territorial (see pages 50–51) and are happiest surrounded by familiar scents and a clear view of what is going on.

Happy cat tip

Cats do not naturally eat together as a social group, unless they live in feral communities and have sufficient food resources. Domestic cats can find it stressful to feed close to one another. Providing separate feeding bowls with adequate space between them for your cats to be able to eat and observe each other at the same time will help to keep them much happier and maintain harmony in the group.

Good boy!

Rewarding good behaviour is the best way to motivate your cat and encourage him to repeat desirable actions, such as using the litter tray when he is supposed to or scratching at the post you've provided rather than the leg of the sofa.

A cat will lap up attention from his owner when he thinks you have noticed how wonderful he is. But what's the best way to praise your cat and make him really happy?

Food

As a special treat you can provide your cat with a few delicacies you know he will enjoy, such as fresh prawns or cooked chicken. Commercial cat treats are available, but don't forget to count these in when calculating your cat's daily intake or he could soon begin to pile on weight (see pages 60–61).

Food rewards can be useful for praising a cat that has done something you are pleased about, or to help train him to do something specific, such as go in a pet carrier. However, don't rely solely on food treats as rewards – there are other ways to let your cat know you're happy with him.

Well done!

Vocal tone is an excellent way of rewarding your cat. The more you talk to him, the more he will 'talk' back to you, using body language and his own vocal sounds (see pages 12–13). When you are happy with your cat, use a slightly higher tone of voice to say 'Good boy', and when you are unhappy – perhaps because he has jumped up onto

furniture you don't want him on – use a slightly deeper, firmer tone of voice to say 'No!' before physically lifting him down.

Games and toys

Your cat will enjoy the attention of playing games with you and this is an invaluable way of making him happy. Homemade toys such as scrunched-up paper, are just as exciting to him as elaborate store-bought items.

The important thing is to spend quality time together, having fun and finding out what types of games he enjoys most (see pages 110–117). Perhaps he prefers squeaky toys, or fishing-rod type games where he has to leap and dive in order to 'catch' his prey. The more time you spend together, the more you will strengthen the relationship between you.

Stroking

Many cats enjoy being handled, whether this is a quick stroke on the head or a full body massage, but watch your pet's body language so that you know when he has had enough (see pages 96–97). However, if your cat is never happier than when he is being given a cuddle, this can be a mutually enjoyable activity that will reduce your stress levels as well as make your cat happy.

2 Is your cat happy?

There are some basic things that all cats need in order to survive. But, as with people, there is a difference between merely surviving and being genuinely content.

In order to have a contented cat, you will need to provide the basics but also all those little extras, many of which cost very little but will make a huge difference to his quality of life.

Back to basics

Food Cats are carnivores and a high-quality diet containing meat is essential for them to maintain optimum health.

Water Constant access to fresh water is essential. Some cats seem to enjoy drinking from puddles and ponds, but they should also have access to indoor water bowls.

Exercise Opportunities to explore and burn off energy help to keep cats physically healthy and mentally stimulated.

Shelter Cats are creatures of comfort and need to be able to escape from the cold and take refuge from the heat when necessary.

Happiness essentials

Sufficient resources Unlike dogs, cats are not naturally pack animals and do not usually appreciate sharing food bowls or litter trays.

Companionship Well-socialized cats will enjoy the attention of their owners and it is important to spend quality time with your pet. If you work all day, it is better to have two cats to entertain each other, as long as they get along well (see pages 32–33).

Socializing Hopefully, your cat has come from a background where he experienced family life and can cope with household activities and meeting new people. An ongoing socialization programme will increase his confidence.

Training Consistency in your house rules will give your cat confidence and prevent him becoming confused as to what he is and isn't allowed to do. Training him to accept handling, enjoy grooming and so on is also essential to his wellbeing.

Routine Cats are creatures of habit and dislike change, particularly as they get older. Reduce your pet's stress levels by making changes gradually.

Veterinary care Providing your cat with regular preventative and reactive health care will help to ensure he has a long and healthy life.

Healthy, happy cat

Providing your cat with basic health care will help to ensure he stays fit and happy. Finding a cat-friendly vet and taking your pet for his annual medical check-up and vaccination boosters will go a long way towards keeping him healthy.

An annual check-up as a matter of routine will also allow early detection and treatment of any problems, even if your cat appears to you to be completely healthy.

Happy cat tip
You can help to make visits to the vet a calm and happy experience by taking your cat's favourite blanket, toys and treats with him. Accustom him to being examined (see pages 84–85) and if necessary schedule some 'fun' visits where you take him to the surgery, sit calmly in the waiting room and then go home again.

Vaccinations
Vaccinating your cat against potentially life-threatening diseases is the single most important thing you need to do to protect him from serious illness. You should not let your cat outside until at

least one week after completing his vaccination course, to allow time for his immunity to build up. Your vet can advise you on this.

Essential vaccines include feline viral rhinotracheitis (cat flu) and feline panleukopenia (distemper), which is particularly dangerous for kittens and young cats. Feline leukaemia (FeLV) is another core vaccine for outdoor cats, particularly prolific hunters. Unfortunately, once a cat is infected with FeLV he remains so for life and will usually go on to develop the fatal disease.

Worming
Cats are vulnerable to internal parasite infestation, and regular preventative treatments are essential. For more information on worm infestations and treatments, see pages 78–79.

Flea treatments
Feline flea infestation is the most common reason vets are consulted by cat owners. Fleas bite the cat's skin and transmit bacteria that can cause skin irritations, infections, hair loss, discomfort and allergic reactions. For more information on flea infestations and treatments, see pages 78–79.

Identification
Microchipping is an invaluable means of permanent identification and will greatly enhance your chances of a happy reunion should your cat go missing. This relatively inexpensive, one-off procedure involves injecting a tiny microchip beneath the skin between the shoulder blades which carries a personal ID number that is linked to a database containing the owner's contact details. A scanner will detect the chip and most rescue centres, charities and veterinary clinics now use these as a matter of course.

Annual check-up
When your cat has his annual booster vaccinations, your vet can also perform a check-up to detect the early onset of any problems. Your cat will be weighed, physically examined from head to tail, the internal organs will be palpated, the teeth inspected, and his heart and lungs checked with a stethoscope. Some cats can be very stalwart about tolerating pain and discomfort, and you may be unaware of problems until your vet discovers them, so it really is worth having these checks carried out annually.

For more information on when your cat should visit the vet and what for, see pages 72–73.

Make visits to the vet relaxed and happy for your cat

Food, glorious food!

In recent years, increased research into feline nutrition has helped to improve the health and longevity of cats. There are so many different types of cat food available that it can be bewildering trying to choose one to keep your cat happy and content.

Every supermarket and pet store stocks a massive variety of cat foods. There are sachets, cans, brand names, supermarket own brands, economy ranges, chunks, dry and wet foods. Then of course there are adult foods, senior foods, kitten foods, light foods and convalescent foods. So, which is best?

Wet or dry?

If you have just acquired a cat or kitten, for the first few weeks use the same food as the breeder or rescue centre from which you got him and introduce any changes gradually to avoid the risk of gastric upset. Thereafter, it is really a matter of personal preference as to whether you feed wet or dry food, or a combination of both. The important thing is to ensure that your cat receives all the nutrition he needs to enjoy optimum health.

Meat please

Do not be tempted to put your cat on a vegetarian diet. To remain healthy cats require the amino acid taurine, which is found almost exclusively in meat. Deficiency can have serious health consequences, including damage to the heart and eyes.

If you are feeding your cat non-commercial food, don't give him liver too often as this has a high vitamin A content, which can be harmful to cats (see pages 62–63). By feeding a commercially prepared cat food you will ensure your cat receives all the nutrients he needs, in the correct quantities.

Kittens and cats

At the age of eight weeks a kitten requires food up to four times a day, and feeding good-quality kitten food will ensure he receives the high-energy diet that his delicate digestive system can manage. As a kitten matures into adulthood, his growth rate slows and he will require fewer calories (particularly after neutering, see pages 76–77) and just two meals a day, morning and evening. Make the transition from kitten to adult cat food very gradually, between the ages of seven and ten months.

RESEARCH

Studies show that cats have complex and very specific dietary requirements, and any nutritional deficiency produces adverse effects very quickly. For example, to enable cats to synthesize urea (a waste product resulting from protein breakdown), cats require the amino acid arginine. Missing just one meal containing arginine results in symptoms such as lethargy, hypersalivation and excessive vocalization.

Complete foods

Check the labelling on cat food to make sure that it is 'complete', which means it contains everything your cat requires in the correct proportions and you need only supply fresh water to ensure he is fed properly. If a food is not labelled as 'complete', you will need to provide additional complementary foods in order for your cat to receive all the nutrition he requires. If you are unsure about your cat's food intake, consult your vet for dietary advice.

Exercise and play

Cats are renowned for the speed and elegance of their movements, and few things are more pleasurable than seeing your pet in full flight as he runs around the garden chasing a leaf or butterfly. Indoor cats can still have fun on activity centres or playing with interactive toys.

Providing your cat with daily opportunities for exercise and play is vital for his happiness. Play and exercise contribute to a cat's contentment by providing mental stimulation, encouraging mobility and burning off excess energy. For kittens, play is essential in developing social, interactive skills and more refined movements, such as manipulating a toy and throwing it in the air as they would do with prey. It also increases eye–paw coordination. For an adult cat, if he is confined indoors (and particularly if he lives alone) play can sometimes be the only aerobic exercise he gets and will help him to maintain his ideal weight or lose a little if necessary.

Timing

Cats are usually more inclined to play around dawn and dusk (see pages 16–17). If you are trying to keep your cat inside in order to protect wildlife, you may find that he will be interested in playing different games at these times.

Leaving toys around the house for your cat to discover will not generally grab his attention, as it is the movement of the toys that motivates him. You will have to 'breathe life' into his toys by throwing, rolling, dragging or hiding them in order to activate his hunting instinct and encourage him to engage in play.

Bored = unhappy

Bored, lonely or unhappy cats tend to manifest their distress in different ways. Some may go off their food, while others exhibit behaviours that are problematic to their owners, such as self-mutilation, excessive vocalization, scratching the furniture, climbing the curtains or toileting in inappropriate places.

Providing your cat with human or feline companionship, enriching his environment, scheduling extra play sessions and offering extra attention, such as grooming, can all help to turn a sour puss into a contented cat once more.

Variety is the spice of life

A tall activity centre, which encourages your cat to climb and perch, will increase his sense of 'territory' and allow him to view his surroundings from a safe spot. Setting up cat perches around

the house and allowing access to windowsills will help to enrich your pet's life. Putting out different toys each day and keeping some back for another time, will also help to provide that random interest factor which is so important to your cat's general wellbeing.

For more information on providing your cat with plenty of attention and fun, see Chapters 6 and 7.

Happy relationships

Cats are often perceived as aloof, elusive creatures, and as a result when they are affectionate with their owners, the relationship seems more meaningful and special.

However, do you really know how your cat views you, and other cats? And what can you do to make the relationship between you even happier?

Too much love

In today's world, many busy people do not have much time to form meaningful relationships with friends, partners or children, and an increasing number of us live alone. A cat can sometimes assume some of these roles, as his owner (consciously or unconsciously) uses him as a baby substitute or confidant.

However, it is a lot to expect of a cat to fulfil his owner's emotional needs, and smothering him with attention can result in over-dependence. An over-dependent cat is ultimately unhappy as he will suffer anxiety when parted from his owner, which can result in behaviour problems or severe disruption of the owner's lifestyle.

To avoid your cat becoming over-dependent on you try to:

- Accustom him to being left alone for short periods.
- Ignore increased demands for affection, rewarding him only when he is quiet.
- Give your cat his own bed to sleep in, away from your bedroom.
- Avoid projecting your anxieties about separation onto your cat. For example, don't make a big fuss of the cat every time you leave him and return. Try to act normally even if you do feel a little anxious.
- Establish a daily routine to help your cat feel secure but don't worry if occasionally you are a few minutes late. Over-dependence on routines can be as psychologically harmful as no routine at all.
- Encourage other family members and visitors to pet the cat and give him treats, so he builds up positive associations with other people, too.

Happy cat tip

Be aware of your cat's calming presence in the house. Learn to breathe deeply and relax when you are stressed, and you will both be much happier!

Mirror, mirror...

Some cats appear oblivious to the moods of their owner, while others are so sensitive and astute that they pick up on emotions and mirror them back. So, if you are stressed or angry your cat may recognize this and act accordingly. Many behaviour 'problems' can be the result of an unhappy cat trying to cope with an intolerable emotional situation.

Territorial rights

Cats are territorial creatures and can easily feel threatened if a strange cat comes into their garden or home. Some cats become aggressive if a new cat moves into the neighbourhood, others become timid, and some flatly refuse to go outside any more! If your cat suddenly changes personality, it may be worth finding out if a new cat has moved into the area and taking steps to persuade him that your cat's garden is not the best place to be (see pages 50–51).

One cat or two?

Cats are so adorable to have around that it is tempting to think how much happier life could be if you had more than one. But would sharing your life with another cat make your existing cat more contented? Or is a solitary life with one-to-one attention from you the best way to keep him happy?

There are few things more heart-warming than seeing two or more cats curled up happily and enjoying a snooze together. However, as with everything, there are pros and cons to having more than one cat in your home. It is worth considering these before you decide to invest in a feline companion for a solo cat.

RESEARCH

A study by the American Pet Product Manufacturers' Association reveals that on average cat owners have 2.4 cats each, and almost three-quarters of all cats living in the USA reside in multi-cat homes.

Pros

✔ Having more than one cat means they can provide entertainment for each other if you are out at work all day.

✔ Cats have varying personalities, and you can enjoy discovering their differences and developing a relationship with more than one individual.

✔ Domestic cats can be social creatures and enjoy the company of their own kind.

Cons

✘ You will incur double the cost in veterinary bills, food, boarding fees and so on.

✘ Some cats find living in a group stressful, and your existing cat could become very unhappy.

✘ Cats that bond with each other may have less of a bond with their owner.

✘ There is a higher risk of undesirable behaviours such as urine marking (see pages 80–81) in a multi-cat household.

Can you cope?

Do your homework, and be honest about whether you have sufficient time, money and other resources to ensure you can provide more than one cat with a happy life. Each cat will need his own feeding bowl, litter tray, bed, hiding places and observation posts, plus opportunities for play, exercise and interaction with you. That can take up a lot of time, space in your house and energy from you. From a financial point of view, investigate veterinary charges, insurance, boarding fees and so on and then budget for them, adding a contingency fund on top to cope with any emergencies.

Happy cat tip

For cats to be happy living in a group, it is best not to put those with extreme personality types together. For example, two over-friendly cats (or kittens) could start competing for your attention, or two very shy cats might prefer each other's company to yours. Try to get cats with 'middle of the road' personalities. When choosing kittens, observe how they behave and ask the breeder to describe their personalities to you.

Slowly does it

The key to cats living together in harmony is to introduce the newcomer to your existing cat slowly, and provide sufficient 'bolt holes' (such as behind a chair) and high perches (perhaps on top of a cupboard) for them to be able to get away from each other if and when the need arises. Separate feeding stations, plus multiple litter trays and other resources, will help to ensure that your cats live together happily.

Pedigree or crossbreed?

Budget and personal preference are the usual indicators that help an owner decide which cat to buy. Some people have childhood dreams of owning a particular breed, while others are happy to cuddle up with an affectionate crossbreed that may not always be as pretty but is entirely loving.

RESEARCH

A survey by the Pet Food Manufacturers' Association reveals that 92 per cent of all cats in the UK are non-pedigree. Black-and-white and tabby are the most common colours. One study shows that pedigree cats are perceived by their owners to be generally more active, less aloof and better tempered than crossbreeds. However, crossbreeds enjoy interacting with their owners in games such as retrieving just as much as pedigree cats (see pages 114–115).

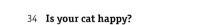

Do we actually know which cats are happiest, and how we can make their lives better? And how can you enjoy life with your pet while still making time to attend to all his needs?

The cat for you

There are pros and cons for deciding whether to go for a pedigree cat or one of unknown breeding. One thing is certain: there is a cat out there to suit everyone. You can get cats with short hair, medium hair, long hair and even no hair... and as for colours, an entire rainbow of beautiful shades and patterns has been developed. For information on matching cat and owner personalities, see pages 36–37.

Happy pedigrees

Some breeds are high maintenance in terms of their physical care and will become very unhappy if you fail to look after them properly each day. For example, a Persian needs daily grooming, which some owners find very relaxing and enjoyable while others consider it a chore. Determining whether or not you can cope with this type of commitment is important before you buy.

Other cats are high maintenance in terms of their demands for your attention. A Siamese, for example, can be quite vocal and his non-stop, live-wire activities may be very entertaining or wear you down, depending on your personality.

Happy crossbreeds

Unlike pedigree cats, which can be expensive and have waiting lists of potential purchasers, crossbreeds cost less to buy and are readily available. The disadvantages are that if one or neither of the cat's parents can be seen, you will have no idea what type of cat the kitten will grow into, and little indication as to his possible personality traits or clues to potential future health problems.

Pedigree kittens and cats are fully vaccinated against disease and come complete with a full family history, so you know exactly what type of cat you are getting. However, some people love the idea of having a totally unique cat, and there is no evidence that crossbreeds are any less loving or happy than one of their pedigree cousins, provided all their feline needs are catered for.

> ### Happy cat tip
> Research the physical requirements of each breed before you commit to buying. Knowing you have chosen a cat you can cope with happily will ensure you have a long and harmonious relationship together.

Cat personalities

The chances are that if you already have a cat, he will have trained you to love and look after him so that all his needs are well catered for. However, if you are still considering getting a cat, taking time to match your personalities will make life much easier and more enjoyable for you both.

Finding a cat that is most likely to live up to your expectations in terms of personality and behaviour will get your relationship off to the best possible start.

Did you know?

The personality of your kitten's parents will help to influence how your kitten is likely to behave. Behaviourists have found that a cat's father has a big influence on the kitten's personality type and behaviour traits, even if he has very little (or no) contact with his offspring. For example, a shy, nervous father will probably produce a shy, nervous kitten, although the mother's behaviour will also help to determine character. This is why it is useful to have knowledge of a kitten's parents, although with a crossbreed this is not always possible (see pages 34–35).

Breed characters

Many people are attracted to a particular breed of pedigree cat because of its personality. There are always exceptions to the rules, but here is a general guide to the most popular breeds:

Abyssinian Gentle, very loyal.

Asian Shorthair Intelligent, curious, less demanding than a Burmese.

Balinese Lively, intelligent, less demanding than a Siamese.

Bengal Athletic, playful, confident.

Birman Intelligent, gentle, quiet.

British Shorthair Friendly and affectionate (see left).

Burmese Outgoing, energetic, enjoys human attention.

Devon and Cornish Rex Playful, energetic, intelligent.

Egyptian Mau Playful, loving.

Exotic Shorthair Gentle, undemanding – similar to a Persian.

Korat Quiet, sweet-natured, intelligent, playful.

Maine Coon Gentle, friendly.

Norwegian Forest Great climber and hunter, independent, friendly.

Oriental Shorthair Intelligent, energetic, loyal, can become very attached to their owner.

Persian Gentle giant, affectionate, placid.

Ragdoll Gentle, affectionate, enjoys being handled (see right).

Russian Blue Quiet, gentle, affectionate.

Siamese Vocal, intelligent, demanding, often with dog-like personality traits.

Somali Intelligent, active.

Tonkinese Intelligent, fun loving, enjoys interactive play.

Social animals

The degree to which a kitten is exposed to people during the first seven weeks of his life will determine how well he can cope with living in a family situation. The more he is socialized, the happier he will be. With pedigree cats, a responsible breeder will ensure that such socialization is carried out thoroughly. Feral kittens that have no contact with people during this time are very difficult to tame and are usually distrustful and unhappy with human contact. For more details on how to socialize your cat, see pages 122–123.

> ## Happy cat tip
> Longhaired and semi-longhaired cats are generally more placid and less demanding than shorthair cats, which are considered to be more lively and energetic. However, you will have to spend additional time grooming a longhaired cat to keep him happy, which is time consuming.

3 Indoors or out?

Whether you keep your cat indoors or out will have a major influence on his happiness and the quality of his life. Indoor cats provided with an interesting and varied environment can be happy and live longer, while outdoor cats enjoy freedom but may be prone to disease, theft and accidents.

Getting the balance right between indoors and out is an important key to your cat's happy life.

Do you have a choice?

Many breeders will refuse to sell a cat unless he will be kept indoors. Pedigrees are expensive and may be stolen; they may not be streetwise, so vulnerable to injury from other cats or traffic. The location of your home – perhaps it is a high-rise apartment or near a busy road – can influence your decision. Providing an outdoor cat run is a good compromise (see pages 104–105).

Keeping an indoor cat happy

Keeping cats indoors provides them with an unnatural lifestyle. Indoor cats need more attention to keep them happy and prevent boredom or undesirable behaviours such as indoor spraying or scratching furniture. There are many ways to enrich the life of an indoor cat and it is vital to do so.

To keep your indoor cat happy he will need:

Activity centre This will encourage him to play, climb and observe the house from different levels, increasing his sense of territory.

Regular play Schedule regular, quality play sessions with you and other family members, to help stimulate your cat and prevent boredom.

Grooming This close contact will enhance the bond between you.

Daily challenges Give your cat problems to solve, such as food puzzles (see pages 110–111) or hidden toys.

Toys Provide a wide variety and rotate them regularly to keep him interested.

Access to fresh grass Your cat will like access to a windowbox of fresh grass. There is some evidence that eating grass helps cats to regurgitate hairballs.

Birdwatching Access to a window will offer your cat the opportunity to enjoy a spot of birdwatching.

Recreation Leaving the radio on while you are out will help to break the monotony. You can buy cat-friendly DVDs of birds, wildlife or fish swimming!

The cat-friendly house

Taking time to look around your home as if from your cat's point of view, will help you to decide which areas can be improved to make it a safe, happy and interesting place for him to live. This is particularly important prior to bringing a kitten home, as his curiosity can take him into small spaces and dangerous situations.

Let's take a look around the home to see how it can be made more cat friendly, for new kittens or an existing pet.

Kitchen

Appliances Put notices on the doors of your washing machine, oven and tumble drier to ensure they are kept shut, and that people check inside before turning them on. Cats find the warm, dark interiors of these appliances a very attractive place for a nap!

Detergents and chemicals Store all household cleaners in a locked cupboard, out of reach of a curious cat.

Plastic bags We all collect them but take care to keep them away from your cat, who may find them fun to play with but can easily get tangled up or even suffocate. Ingesting plastic can make your cat sick.

Refuse containers Invest in rubbish bins with tight, well-fitting lids and advise everyone to keep the lids on. Avoid swing bins – your cat may try to get inside and then be unable to climb out again.

Living areas

Fire Invest in a strong fire guard to prevent your cat climbing up the chimney and to protect him from being burned. Some cats, particularly older ones, show little common sense when it comes to dozing in front of the fire, and burned whiskers are an unhappy but regular occurrence!

Shelves Clear these of any valuable or sentimental items that your cat may break, particularly when he is an energetic kitten longing to explore his new environment.

Houseplants Check with your garden centre or vet to ensure that any you already have are not toxic to cats if eaten and, if necessary, give them away to a non-cat owning neighbour.

Fish tank Your cat will love watching fish swimming in a tank or bowl, but make sure it has a tight-fitting lid that he can't undo and is placed where there is no risk of him knocking it over.

Tidy up Clear away any small items that may be chewed or eaten by your cat, such as the contents of a sewing box with loose needles and pins.

Bathroom

Shower and bath Keep shower doors closed and never leave a full bath unattended. Some cats can be quite interested in water, particularly if there are lots of pretty bubbles floating on the top. It is easy for him to slide into the water and then be unable to climb out up the slippery sides of the bath.

Toilet Here is an excellent opportunity to teach family members to keep the toilet lid down! A curious cat or kitten can easily fall in.

Medicine cabinet Store all medications in a lockable cabinet. Many human medicines, such as aspirin, are dangerous to cats if eaten.

Windows

To ensure that a curious kitten doesn't climb out of an upstairs window and fall, keep the windows closed. If you want to keep your cat indoors, or prevent neighbouring cats visiting, fit strong mesh screens over the window so that you can safely leave them open.

> ### Happy cat tip
> Putting a child's stairgate in a doorway will allow you to introduce your cat safely to other pets. By providing a barrier, he will be able to get used to their smell and appearance without the risk of an over-boisterous greeting or other frightening experience. You will need to supervise to ensure the cat doesn't jump over the stairgate or squeeze through it.

House rules

Some cats, particularly those belonging to anxious first-time owners, perceive themselves to be the head of the household. Before long, their owners are pandering to their every need and totally neglecting their own lives, and the stress this causes can be considerable. Establishing ground rules will make life easier and your home a happier and calmer place to be.

Research has disproved the theory that cats are always loners and incapable of living in social groups. However, in any group there has to be a leader, so make sure from day one that this is *you*.

Be consistent

A confused cat is an unhappy cat, so be consistent with any rules you make – such as whether or not you allow him onto the furniture – and ensure that everyone in the house knows what they are and complies with them. There is little point in you trying to train the cat not to jump on the sofa if your partner or children encourage him.

Just say 'No'

It is unhygienic to allow cats onto food preparation areas, so discourage this at the first opportunity. If your cat jumps up, say 'No' in a loud, clear voice and lift him down onto the floor immediately. If you do this every time, he will soon get the message that this is a no-go area.

However, the one time you forget, and absent-mindedly give him positive attention such as a quick stroke or a treat, you reinforce the fact that this might be a good place to be. He will then be unable to resist jumping up on another occasion, on the off-chance there might be something rewarding for him there.

When you are not in the kitchen, remove temptation by ensuring all food is stored away safely in the refrigerator or sealed containers.

No kissing!

Discourage your cat from licking you or your children, particularly around the face. Cats carry diseases such as cat scratch fever, ringworm or bacterial infections that can be transferred to people, so it makes sense not to put anyone at risk.

Encourage children to wash their hands after handling the cat, particularly before meals, and wipe tables and food preparation areas regularly with a pet-friendly disinfectant.

And so to bed...

If you are happy with your cat sleeping on your bed, go ahead and let him do so. However, if you want him to sleep in his own bed, encourage this from the beginning. Many cats are quite active at night and you may wish to choose him a room as far from yours as possible to ensure you get a good night's sleep!

Put your cat's bed somewhere warm and draught free, with access to a litter tray and fresh water. Once you are in bed, don't be tempted to get up and play with him or give him attention every time he is vocal. The more you reward attention-seeking behaviour, the harder it will be to establish a happy, peaceful bedtime routine.

Kitties and kids

Children and cats can be a happy combination, provided certain ground rules are followed and mutual respect is established. Children learn most by example, and so the chances are that if they see you handling and talking to your cat kindly, they will too.

From the beginning, explain to children that even though a kitten or cat may look cute, he is not a toy and must be treated with care.

Careful handling

Some cats are more tolerant of children than others, but as a rule they do not enjoy being carried around from room to room. A cat that feels he is being restrained against his will or is being held awkwardly, may struggle or scratch to jump out of your child's arms.

> **RESEARCH**
>
> Studies show that children who are involved with and attached to a pet such as a cat develop higher empathy, learn responsibility earlier and may even have higher IQ scores than children without a pet. Even three- to four-year-old children with pets are better able to understand the feelings of other children than those without. It is thought that because a cat or dog won't always do what the child wants them to, this teaches tolerance and encourages them to look at things from another perspective. The more time a child spends with their pet, the greater impact it has on the child's life.

> **Caution**
>
> If you have a baby in the house, always cover the cot or pram with a well-fitted net that is strong enough to support a cat should he decide to jump into it.

To avoid this, show your child the best way to pick up the cat. He will feel most secure if he is lifted from the front, with one arm under his front legs and the other gently supporting his back legs. Ask the child to sit quietly with him rather than carry him around, and allow the cat to leave when he's had enough.

Happy cats *and* children

- Always supervise young children and cats.
- Encourage respect for the cat and explain he is vulnerable to injury if handled roughly or dropped suddenly.
- Involve children in the cat's daily care – fetching food bowls, filling dishes, learning to groom and so on.
- Give children treats to offer the cat, so that positive associations begin to build up. If the cat is reluctant, ask the child to throw a treat towards him until he overcomes his shyness.
- Explain that a cat should never be disturbed when sleeping or using the litter tray.
- Encourage everyone to wash their hands thoroughly after handling the cat (see pages 42–43).
- Play should be gentle, using toys rather than fingers. Don't encourage a kitten to jump on your fingers or bite them, as this will hurt when he is a fully grown cat. Rough play by the child or cat must signal the end of the game.
- Screaming, over-excited or boisterous children can soon overwhelm a cat. If this happens, put the cat in a quiet room until he settles down.
- Adopt a zero-tolerance approach to physical punishment, explaining how unhappy and frightened this will make the cat.

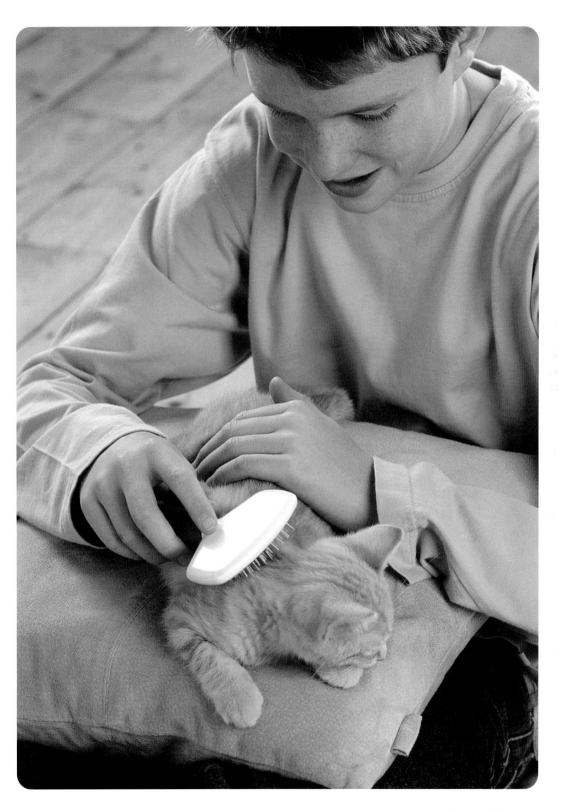

The cat-friendly garden

Allowing your cat access to the garden will open up a whole new world of adventures to him. Cats love to explore, climb and have fun when they are outdoors, all of which contribute to their fitness, wellbeing and happiness.

Happy cat tip
Encourage children to put the lid on their sandpit when it is not in use, as otherwise your cat may be tempted to use it as an alternative litter tray.

However, it is important to ensure that your garden is a safe and pleasant place for your cat to spend time, particularly if he goes out unsupervised. Your vet can advise you on when it is safe to let your cat outside following his course of vaccinations (see pages 24–25).

Preparation

In the meantime, check that your garden is as safe and secure as possible. Examine fencing and repair or replace any loose panels, and if necessary put up solid gates to help to keep out other cats, dogs or foxes and prevent them traumatizing your cat. Ensure that water butts are covered with tight-fitting lids to prevent a curious cat falling inside.

Outdoor toileting

Cats can view flowerbeds as giant litter trays. Some gardeners resort to putting prickly cuttings or pine needles on the borders in the hope of discouraging this, but such deterrents can easily cut paws or become painfully lodged between the pads. To avoid this, designate a quiet, private area of the garden that your cat can use as a toilet – a mound of freshly dug soil or sand is ideal. Take him to this area regularly and praise him when he uses it. Don't forget to clean up as often as you would his indoor litter tray.

Garden must-haves

The four things your cat needs to keep him happy outdoors are: access to fresh water, a sunny spot in which to relax and doze, a shaded area to retreat to and shelter from the cold. Anything else is a bonus, but if you want to enhance your cat's garden experience here are some ideas:

- Plant clumps of bamboo (see pages 102–103) or areas of long, wispy grass for him to wander through and sleep among.
- Provide one or two high observation areas for him to jump up onto and survey the garden.
- Ponds can be dangerous for cats, so consider a pebble water feature. Some cats enjoy drinking from them, or paddling through.

Poisonous plants

Some plants are toxic to cats if eaten. If you are uncertain about any of the plants in your garden, check with your garden centre or vet. For more information on plants to avoid, see pages 102–103.

Free choice

A cat flap allows your cat the ultimate freedom of choosing when he wants to go outside and come back in again. Some flaps are activated by a magnet on the cat's collar, which also keeps other cats out of the house.

Happy hunting

Even though most domestic cats are no longer required to catch mice or small mammals in order to survive, they still maintain a strong hunting instinct. This is deep rooted, but the good news is that there are many ways to keep your cat happy and satisfy his instincts that do not involve hurting a single mouse or bird.

Did you know?

In the wild, cats bring live prey home to enable their kittens to practise their hunting skills. This may be why domestic cats proudly bring home presents of birds or mice for their owners to enjoy! If this happens, try not to shriek in horror, and if you manage to rescue the creature put it in a quiet, dark place to recover until you can safely release it back into the wild.

Encourage your cat to satisfy his hunting skills through play

Even well-fed cats will hunt, although the desire seems to decrease with age. The peak years for hunting are between two and seven. Older cats tend to become less motivated, and more interested in sunbathing than stalking birds. However, there are always exceptions to the rule, and some cats remain active hunters all their lives.

Protecting wildlife

The single most important thing you can do to protect wildlife is to keep your cat indoors around sunrise and sunset, as this is when birds flock and feed and are most vulnerable, and cats are well adapted to huntimg (see pages 14–15).

A cat will often hide in long grass or shrubbery to watch wildlife, sometimes moving a step or two closer and then freezing again. As soon as the unsuspecting prey moves close enough, he will pounce. Always site bird tables or feeders in open areas on high poles, so that the birds can see a stalking cat easily and take off quickly. Avoid areas overhung with trees, which will enable a cat to hide and pounce more easily.

Playtime

Encourage your cat to satisfy his hunting skills through play (see pages 114–115). Attaching a toy to a piece of string and dragging it along for him to stalk and pounce on is a good example. Fixing long feathers or a bird toy to a stick and waving it up and down will encourage your cat to jump up and practise his bird-catching skills. Games such as these are also good exercise, excellent for coordination and will help to keep his figure in great shape.

Space invaders

Cats are territorial creatures and have little respect for human boundaries such as garden gates or fences. Problems can occur when one cat encroaches on another's perceived territory, and unhappy cats can develop all kinds of behaviour problems.

RESEARCH
Studies of domestic cats have shown that a male cat's home range (the area he normally inhabits) is three to ten times larger than that of a female. This means that male cats will often wander through neighbouring gardens quite happily. A female, on the other hand, is generally happy to spend most of her time in her owner's garden, or just beyond.

It is important to understand how your cat views his territory in order to keep him happy, both indoors and out.

Territory marking

A cat's territory is the area that he will defend against other cats. Territories are usually slightly smaller than the cat's normal home range (see Research). Depositing faeces is a key method used by cats to mark their territory and, contrary to popular belief, they will do this in their own garden as well as on the border of neighbouring land. Finding uncovered cat faeces on your lawn or flowerbed does not mean your cat is being lazy – it is a sign that he feels territorially challenged by other cats in the area.

Cats in multi-cat households, or those in neighbourhoods where there are a high number of cats, are more prone to experiencing territorial stress. This is often manifested in behaviours such as inappropriate soiling or spraying. Providing every cat with access to retreats, hiding places and observation posts, and increasing the number of feeding bowls, litter trays and so on to prevent bullying over resources, will help the cats to feel more secure.

Home on the range

Research shows that cats living in rural areas have larger home ranges than those in outer suburbia, while those in areas that are densely populated by both people and other cats have the smallest ranges of all. The smaller a cat's range, the more likely it is that another cat will encroach on his territory, causing the resident cat to feel defensive and insecure.

If your cat is frightened by the presence of another cat entering his garden, a well-aimed squirt from a water pistol may deter the unwanted visitor and help him to view your garden as an unwelcome place. This will be even more effective if you are able to hide and take aim from an upstairs window, as this way the intruder will associate the unpleasant experience with entering your garden rather than you.

Ensure your cat has access to a cat flap that only he can get through (see pages 46–47), should he wish to escape in a hurry.

Be considerate

If your cat is the local neighbourhood bully, try to only let him out when your neighbour's cat is likely to be indoors to avoid confrontation. Giving him a collar with a bell (see pages 48–49) can help to alert other cats to his presence, so that they can make a swift exit.

Happy cat tip

The more attractive and welcoming you can make your own garden, the happier your cat will be to stay in it and the less likely he is to wander off to explore another cat's territory. In addition, the more time you spend in different parts of your garden with your cat, playing games, gardening or simply sitting in a chair, the more he will recognize that this is 'his' space where he can feel happy and secure.

Outdoor training

Taking time to teach your cat to come back when you call him, will give you great peace of mind when he is enjoying himself out in the garden. However, if you would feel happier having a little more control over your cat's movements, walking on a harness may be the best solution.

Either of these options will allow you to provide your cat with more time outside, which will definitely help to keep him happier.

Come back!

Don't wait until your cat goes outside for the first time to teach him the recall command. Begin when he is a tiny kitten, or as soon as you get him home.

Get into the habit of carrying some tasty cat treats with you at all times, perhaps in a waist pouch or in a bag in your pocket. When your cat is already walking towards you of his own accord, say his name and offer him a treat as soon as he gets to you. Repeat this several times a day and encourage other family members to do the same, so that your cat learns his name – particularly important if you have changed it for some reason – and begins to make positive associations with returning to his owners.

Never get cross or irritated with your cat if he doesn't come when you call him, as this will put him off complying the next time you want him to come. Instead, make the treats you offer higher

value and the praise even more enthusiastic, so that he finds you much more interesting than anything he was doing beforehand.

Harness training

Begin by accustoming your cat to wearing a comfortable, well-fitting harness for a few minutes each day in the house. Remain calm and confident when you put the harness on, and offer him something tasty, such as cooked prawns, as a distraction. Begin with just a minute or two of wearing the harness and gradually progress to longer periods.

When your cat accepts the harness easily, you can then attach the lead and tempt him to follow you using food treats or a toy as a lure. Again, progress slowly, walking around the house at first before venturing outside. Allow your cat to stop and sniff anything that interests him and don't get into confrontations where you are trying to pull him along. Ignore any behaviour you don't want, distracting and encouraging him with treats and praise.

RESEARCH

Behaviourists have observed that many cats appear to enjoy the attention and stimulation associated with training. Cats can be taught a variety of 'tricks', such as to sit, shake a paw or even open a door. Research shows that encouraging and rewarding positive behaviour is the best way to train a cat.

Home alone

It is unrealistic to think you can be at home with your cat all day, every day. Many working owners have no choice but to leave their cat alone for several hours at least, on most days of the week.

However, while you are away there is a lot you can do to make sure your home-alone cat is happy.

I'm bored

Left entirely to his own devices and without any entertainment, a cat will quickly become bored. When you come home, you may find evidence of this in the form of scratched furniture, chewed clothes, overturned bins and so on. Some cats self-harm by excessive grooming or pulling their fur out in clumps, while others refuse to use their litter tray.

Thinking up ways to allow your cat to indulge in natural feline behaviours, such as climbing, hunting and observing, will be time and energy well spent.

Toys

Provide your cat with a variety of toys and swap these around so that he has something different to do each day. Cats love toys that move unpredictably, in the way prey does. Tying bouncy or squeaky toys on elastic to doorframes, activity centres or scratch posts will help to keep him entertained. For more information on toys, see pages 110–113.

Activity centres

Cats love climbing and providing an activity centre is a great way of encouraging this. It will help to keep your cat fit and active, and will increase the space available to him.

The simplest activity centres consist of a sturdy carpet-covered tube with one or two observation platforms, while more elaborate designs can be so large as to take up almost an entire room in your house. The best include tunnels, hiding places and shelves. To get exactly what you want for your cat, you could commission a local carpenter to make one to your own specification.

In addition, allowing your cat access to high perches within the home will help to make him more confident and secure, and encourage him to explore. Hiding the odd treat on top of a bookcase or shelf will help keep him interested.

Scratch posts

Cats need to scratch to remove the outer claw sheath, sharpen their claws and release pheromones that make them feel secure, confident and happy. Experiment until you find a scratch post that your cat likes. Some prefer natural wood, while others enjoy sinking their claws into carpeting or sisal. For more information on scratch posts, see pages 106–107.

Sunshine and fresh air

Your cat will appreciate having some areas where he can sunbathe and experience fresh air. Leaving a mesh-covered window open provides him with

Happy cat tip

Once positioned, try not to move your cat's scratch post as he will feel happier and more secure if it is always in the same place.

different smells and sensations, and hanging a bird feeder in a nearby tree where your cat can see it will provide extra interest. He may feel a little frustrated, but he certainly won't be bored!

Food

Keep your cat happy with an automatic feeder that dispenses a small amount of food every couple of hours. You can also buy or make food puzzles to help keep him occupied (see pages 110–111). Working for his food will help to simulate more natural eating, keep your cat occupied for longer and provide him with extra exercise.

Home again

When you get home, don't just ignore your cat, get changed and dash out again. Imagine how unhappy you would be if someone did that to you after you'd been home alone all day! Always spend some quality time with your cat.

Harmony in the home

It can be great fun to have two or more cats, provided they all get on well as a group and enjoy each other's company. Maintaining harmony in a multi-cat household takes a little forward planning and organization, but the benefits are well worth the effort.

Many domestic cats are more than capable of being sociable and living in a small group, but asking them to live in cramped conditions with insufficient feeding stations and litter trays or places to hide from suspected aggressors will result in unhappy cats. Although some multi-cat households seem harmonious, others are at best homes where the cats simply tolerate each other.

Two's company

If your kitten is going to be an indoor cat, he will be much happier with another kitten as a companion. Siblings with similar temperaments and preferably tolerant, confident personalities often get on better, and getting two kittens at the same time is much easier than introducing a second one later on.

However, even kittens and cats that get along well still need to be able to retreat from each other when they want to. Providing them with bolt holes such as the back of a sofa, top of a cupboard or a shelf will help them to feel happier.

Three's a crowd?

There are no set rules as to how much room a cat needs in order to be happy, but common sense should apply. Two cats can often get along, but three may result in one being bullied. Some pedigree breeds, such as Siamese or Burmese, are considered more territorial than other, more placid breeds and care must be taken not to overcrowd them.

RESEARCH

Cat food manufacturers recognize that many cats now live in multi-cat households and it is easier for owners to be able to feed one food rather than several different varieties. Extensive research has resulted in the development of some highly nutritious, lower-calorie foods, suitable for indoor cats living in a multi-cat household. Feeding these will keep each cat's weight under control, especially if food is left out and one cat eats more than his fair share, and help to avoid health problems.

Are your cats happy?

Just because your cats are not constantly fighting does not necessarily mean all is well. There are other, more passive ways in which cats demonstrate their distress. For example:

- Over-grooming.
- Indoor spraying.
- Refusing to eat in the same room.
- Guarding of food or doorways.
- Refusing to play with another cat.
- History of cystitis.
- Refusing to come to you if another cat is present.
- Obesity.

To keep your cats happy they will need:

- Beds in different areas of the house.
- A balanced diet (make sure each cat is eating his full share).
- One feeding bowl per cat, plus one extra (so a clean bowl is always available if needed).
- One litter tray per cat positioned in quiet, private areas, plus one extra (as above).
- Extra water bowls.
- High observation posts.
- Areas to which they can retreat.
- Mental and physical stimulation.
- Equal attention from you.

4 Fit or fat?

A key factor in any cat's health and fitness is his diet. This chapter will help you understand more about what your cat needs to eat every day in order to keep him happy and healthy, and whether or not he needs any additional supplements.

Understanding how your cat's digestive system functions will help you to realize the importance of each stage of the food's journey.

The food journey

Mouth and teeth Adult cats have 30 teeth, designed for catching and killing their prey, then tearing it into chunks and swallowing it. Problems with gums and teeth are one of the primary reasons cats are taken to the vet, often when the cat's mouth is so sore that he has stopped eating. Checking your cat's mouth regularly can help you to detect problems early (see pages 82–83).

Gullet Food travels down the oesophagus (gullet) rapidly, so the only problem likely to occur here is if the cat swallows a foreign body that may get stuck and require medical intervention.

Stomach The muscular bag that forms a cat's stomach is lined with strong acids to kill off harmful bacteria and break down the food. As the cat eats, food is stored in the stomach and released in small, regular amounts to the lower digestive tract (intestines). Vomiting can be a sign that there are problems in the stomach.

Liver and pancreas The liver and pancreas are not part of the digestive tract but are involved in the digestive system. They have many roles: in particular, the liver produces bile and the pancreas insulin.

Small intestine This is a long, tubular structure lined with glands to digest and absorb food. Intestinal disorders have a wide range of symptoms including watery diarrhoea and incontinence.

Large intestine This consists of two parts. Digested food passes through the colon, where water is absorbed from it back into the body, and waste matter is then excreted via the rectum. Disorders of the large intestine include colitis (inflammation of the colon), which can cause diarrhoea.

A fat cat is not a happy cat

Overweight or obese cats are at increased risk of developing debilitating and life-shortening conditions such as arthritis, diabetes, respiratory problems and a compromised immune system. The risk of a cat becoming overweight increases as he becomes older and less active.

RESEARCH
Studies show that feral cats typically eat between 10 and 20 small meals per day, with much of the time between meals spent foraging. Behaviourists have found that simulating this behaviour in domestic cats by providing food puzzles (see pages 110–111), hiding food for the cat to find and throwing dry food for the cat to chase and 'hunt down' provides good exercise, and helps to prevent obesity and behaviour problems.

You should be able to notice if your cat is putting on extra weight: he will probably have piled on fat around his ribs, back or underneath his belly. Of course, if he can no longer fit through the cat flap, jump onto his favourite chair or has difficulty keeping himself clean, then it's definitely time to take action!

Weight checks

Your vet will weigh your cat during his annual health check (see pages 24–25) and inform you if he thinks he is overweight, but by weighing your cat once a month and making a note of the results you can monitor the situation more regularly. The simplest method of weighing a cat is to put his carrier on the scales and see how much that weighs, then pop the cat inside and do your sums.

Slowly does it

Just as with humans, the only way for your cat to lose weight is to reduce his calorie intake and increase his physical activity. He will only lose weight if he is burning more energy than he is gaining from his food. However, it is important not to put your cat on a strict diet overnight, but to make any changes gradually. Ask your vet if they have a feline weight-loss clinic you can attend with your cat, or a programme to follow. Many owners cannot believe how much happier and more active their cats become once they have dropped their excess weight.

Play with your cat more, to encourage him to be more active

Top weight-loss tips

- Always feed the recommended allowances of cat food. Don't guess at the amount – weigh it out using scales.
- If you tend to be over-generous, buy your cat a smaller food bowl.
- Cut out food treats and replace with extra praise, toys and attention.
- Play with your cat more, to encourage him to be more active.
- Retain a few pieces of food from your cat's daily allowance to use as treats.
- Feed your cat three or four small meals rather than two large ones each day. But don't increase the amount!
- Put some dry food into a food puzzle (see pages 110–111) so that the cat has to work to get it out, and will use up some calories.
- Ensure that everyone in the family is fully informed of your cat's weight-loss programme so that nobody is tempted to give in to his demands for extra food.

Hidden extras

In today's hectic and often polluted world, many of us feel we need extra supplements and additives to top up the nutrients in our food and keep us healthy. Perhaps our cats also need a little extra help from time to time.

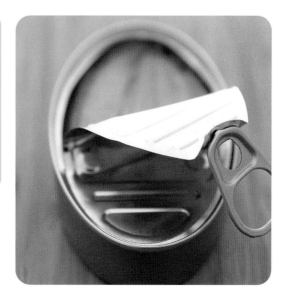

Happy cat tip

Once weaned, all cats are intolerant of the lactose contained in cow's milk and should not be offered it as this can result in gastric upsets. If you really want to be sure that your cat 'gets the cream', feed him a commercially prepared cat or kitten milk (available from supermarkets and pet stores).

Supermarkets and pet stores stock a bewildering array of liquids, tablets and tonics you may be tempted buy for your cat, but can they really make him any happier?

Additives

It is now possible to buy commercially prepared cat food that has been made without any extra artificial additives, although it is not always clear whether some of the ingredients used are themselves completely additive free. If you have a cat that is food sensitive you may find he is happier on this type of diet, although it can be more expensive. Always check with your vet before embarking on any dietary changes, and make sure these are introduced gradually.

Canned food is less likely to contain preservatives, as it is the canning process itself that preserves the food. This is why canned food should be disposed of within a day of opening and kept in the refrigerator with a lid on between feeds.

Dry food is more likely to contain preservatives, and if you buy preservative-free dry food remember that it will not last as long – buy it in smaller quantities and use before the 'use by' date expires. Store all types of dry food in an airtight container with a tightly fitting lid.

Not all additives are harmful, but it is common sense to avoid highly coloured foods. Your cat really won't be unhappy if all his food is sludge brown in colour!

Supplements

When feeding supplements, it is possible to upset the delicate balance of commercially prepared cat food and overdose your pet on certain vitamins and minerals. It is therefore always advisable to seek veterinary advice before feeding any supplements. For pregnant or convalescing cats, your vet may recommend the addition of extra vitamins or minerals, but for healthy cats being fed a complete cat food (see pages 26–27) it may not be necessary to feed any extra supplements.

Your cat's dietary requirements will change as he gets older, and although special senior foods are available (see pages 150–151) your vet may advise supplementing his diet with extra vitamins and minerals – particularly water-soluble B vitamins, which will be flushed out in the urine as the kidneys become less efficient. Many senior foods have additional calcium and sunflower oil to help maintain a shiny coat and healthy gums, teeth and bones.

RESEARCH

Studies show that cats fed on diets consisting mainly of raw liver developed hypervitaminosis A (an excess of vitamin A). Vitamin A is best known for its importance in vision. The daily requirement for an adult cat is 650–850 IU, which can be found in just 5 g (1/6 oz) of good-quality beef liver.

The fussy eater

It is very satisfying to feed a pet you love a delicious meal and watch them enjoy every last morsel. However, if you are the owner of a cat that is finicky about his food, it can be very distressing to buy or prepare meals each day only to find that your cat refuses to eat them.

RESEARCH
Scientists have discovered a genetic reason for cats turning up their nose at sweet, sugary treats that dogs would snap up. Research suggests that the gene that codes part of the cat's sweet-taste receptor and sends information back to his brain works differently in cats, and they cannot actually taste sweet things.

So, how can you go about changing your fussy cat into a happy eater?

Loving too much

You usually end up with the cat you deserve, and over-anxious or over-attentive owners often unconsciously create anxious, attention-seeking cats or fussy eaters.

Although you may think you are being kind, pandering to a cat's every demand for food and even spoon-feeding him when he refuses to eat will simply reinforce the behaviour. In extreme cases, the cat can completely take over your life! For example, one behaviourist recalls seeing a client who offered seven different varieties of food to her beloved cat at every single meal, in the hope that she could tempt him to eat a little bit of some of them. This is a classic case of too much 'love', and will make neither him nor you happy.

Healthy and happy

If your cat has always had a healthy appetite and suddenly goes off his food there may be a medical explanation. Get him checked by the vet to ensure all is well before embarking on a healthy-eating programme or change in diet.

Tough love

Once your cat has been given a clean bill of health by the vet, you can begin to implement a new feeding regime to get his eating habits back on

track. Twice a day, put down his allowance of balanced, complete cat food in a clean bowl. If he doesn't eat it, don't try to tempt him by spoon-feeding or offering other tasty snacks and treats. Leave the food down for him for about 20 minutes, calmly removing the bowl at the end of the allotted time and disposing of any uneaten food each night. Behaviourists predict that a cat will start eating properly again within two to three days. Seek veterinary advice if your cat refuses to eat anything at all, and ensure he always has access to fresh water.

If you continue to experience problems with your cat's eating habits, it may be worth asking your vet for a referral to a professional behaviour counsellor. They may pinpoint another stress-related reason for your cat's behaviour and help you to develop a behaviour modification programme to overcome this.

What a treat!

Get creative in the kitchen and make some homemade treats and meals for your cat to enjoy. It can be fun to experiment with different ingredients and find out what your pet considers to be fine feline cuisine.

Tasty treats

You can make a batch of these delicious treats and store them as directed, serving just a small amount each day.

Tuna treats

250 g (8 oz) can tuna in oil
125 g (4 oz) wholemeal flour
125 g (4 oz) cornflour
250 g (4 oz) oatmeal
250 ml (8 fl oz) chicken broth

Place the tuna, flour and oatmeal in a bowl and add enough broth to mix to a firm dough. Roll out on a floured board to 5 mm (¼ in) thickness. Use a small cutter to cut out shapes or a knife to score the dough into squares. Bake in a preheated oven, 160°C (325°F), Gas Mark 3, for 35 minutes, until crisp and fully cooked. Allow to cool before serving and store in an airtight container.

Super salmon pâté

250 g (8 oz) can salmon
125 g (4 oz) fresh breadcrumbs
125 g (4 oz) celery, finely chopped
1 medium egg, beaten
1 sachet unflavoured gelatine
125 ml (8 fl oz) water, or according to gelatine instructions

Combine all the ingredients in a bowl and press firmly into an ovenproof mould or dish. Bake in a preheated oven, 180°C (350°F), Gas Mark 4, for 40 minutes. Turn out onto a plate to cool. Store in the refrigerator and serve at room temperature.

Catty casserole

Make your cat a delicious casserole using one finely chopped chicken breast plus a selection of diced vegetables such as broccoli, carrots and celery (a couple of tablespoons will be sufficient), plus about 60 g (2 oz) brown or white rice. Cover with water or chicken stock and bake in a preheated oven, 180°C (350°F), Gas Mark 4, for about 50 minutes, or until the rice and chicken are cooked.

Unusual flavours

Cats have been known to enjoy tomato paste, chopped parsley, fish oil, yeast extract and brewer's yeast. They also appreciate small amounts of cooked, chopped vegetables, although cats primarily love protein. Check with your vet if your cat is on a special diet or you are unsure whether a particular ingredient is healthy to feed.

Foods to avoid

When choosing ingredients for cat treats, avoid **liver** (see pages 62–63).

Limit how much **tuna** your cat has each week, as the raised levels of mercury contained in some canned tuna may be harmful to cats.

Chocolate contains a chemical called theobromine that is highly toxic to cats (and dogs), and if consumed in large quantities can be fatal.

Other foods to avoid are onions, pork (including bacon), alcohol, full-fat cow's milk, bones (which may splinter), raw fish and raw eggs. All meat should be cooked to eliminate any potentially harmful micro-organisms.

Water works

Cats need to drink water to survive, but quite often an owner hardly ever sees their pet go to his bowl to quench his thirst. Don't worry: provided your cat has access to fresh water, whenever he likes – important if you have more than one cat – the chances are he's sipping away quite happily.

Water is essential for many bodily functions, including transporting materials between tissues, controlling pH and temperature, lubricating tissue cells, balancing electrolytes and helping to prevent dehydration.

How much is enough?

Cats fed on wet food can often get most of the moisture they need from this. The fact is that cats don't need to drink as much as you probably think. Being directly descended from the African wild cat (*Felis sylvestris lybica*), our domestic cats are physiologically adapted to survive in semi-desert conditions.

A cat's system produces urine so concentrated that it manages to preserve as much precious water as possible. In addition, cats do not sweat (except through the pads of their feet) and, as you may have noticed, are adept at resting and conserving their energy during the heat of the day and becoming more active later on when the temperature has dropped.

Troubled waters

Cats fed on dry or semi-moist food will need to drink more, as these foods contain very little moisture. They are more at risk from dehydration as well as kidney and bladder problems, if fed dry food and deprived of water.

Many cats are sensitive to the chemicals used to treat water, or can smell a detergent that has been used to wash their bowl. This may be why some cats prefer to drink from a rain puddle or pond and are quite fastidious, so are unlikely to choose a dirty or polluted source of water. Our human palates are unable to distinguish the subtle differences in flavoured water, but as long as your cat is drinking happily it's fine to allow him to choose his own source.

Happy cat tip

After washing your cat's bowl, rinse it and allow to drip-dry to dissipate any residual detergent. Your cat will be more willing to use it when traces of chemicals are removed.

Did you know?

Your cat's tongue is designed for lapping up fluids, and as he drinks it forms a ladle shape specifically for this purpose. He will lap up several sips of water and then swallow them down in one gulp.

Pampered pet

If you want to pamper your cat, you can buy purified, non-carbonated waters for cats that are enhanced with taurine and calcium, both essential to his health. Alternatively, why not flavour some water yourself with a little chicken gravy or a splash of lactose-free milk (see pages 62–63)?

Heavy drinkers

If your cat suddenly starts to drink excessively, this could indicate an underlying health problem such as kidney disease, thyroid problems or diabetes. Take him to the vet for a physical examination and laboratory tests, so that a diagnosis can be made and treatment commenced.

5 Health and happiness

Your cat's nutritional, physical and emotional needs will change through the various stages of his life. To keep him healthy, you should take into account his age, breed, lifestyle and medical history.

Top tips for health care

- Keep your cat's documentation and vaccination certificates together in a folder so that you can take them with you to each surgery visit.
- Accustom your cat to going in his carrier so that this is not stressful for him (see pages 126–127).
- Keep your vet's telephone number close to the telephone so you do not have to search for it in an emergency.
- Write the date of your cat's annual check-up and booster vaccinations, plus any other routine vet visits, on the family calendar so that you don't miss these important appointments.
- Be aware of your cat's normal eating, sleeping and drinking habits. You will then notice when his habits change, which could signal the onset of illness.
- Don't think you are wasting your vet's time by taking your cat to be examined simply because you have a hunch that something is wrong. As his owner, you are in the best position to know when your cat is happy and in good health, and when he is not.
- Make a note of any questions you want to ask the vet before your visit, so you don't become distracted and forget to voice any concerns.

Signs that your cat may be unwell

- Unexplained changes to appetite or drinking habits.
- Changes to sleep patterns.
- Dull, matted coat.
- Obesity.
- Weight loss.
- Apparent personality changes.
- Litter-tray problems.
- Behaviour problems, such as refusing to go outside.
- Breathing difficulties.
- Coughing and/or runny eyes and nose.
- Spitting out food while eating.
- Foul-smelling breath or ears.
- Diarrhoea or constipation.
- Excessive vocalization.
- Disorientation.
- Scratching and licking the coat excessively.
- Eating non-food items.

Visits to the vet

Your cat should visit the vet at least once a year for his annual check-up and booster vaccinations. However, some practices run additional clinics that may be useful in providing information and advice throughout each stage of your cat's life.

Kitten classes
The happiest cats are those that have been thoroughly socialized in the first months of their lives (see pages 122–123). This means exposing them to different situations, people and environments so that they are able to cope better with the stresses and strains of our busy lives.

Kitten classes are often run by one of the veterinary nurses and are designed to allow kittens to play and socialize with each other in a safe environment. They also enable the owners to ask questions and pick up tips on all aspects of kitten behaviour, health and wellbeing. If your veterinary surgery offers these clinics, sign up and make sure you and your kitten get off to a happy, healthy start together.

Obesity classes
A fat cat is not a happy cat. If by any chance your adult cat becomes overweight, you may be able to take advantage of a feline obesity clinic. Having the support of a veterinary nurse and other owners can often make this process much less stressful for everyone involved (see pages 60–61).

Geriatric classes
As a cat ages his needs will change, and many veterinary surgeries provide clinics specifically for the older feline. Your cat will be examined and weighed, and any relevant issues such as weight loss, lack of mobility or toileting problems, will be addressed. The aim of these clinics is to keep older cats as healthy and happy as possible by detecting problems early and treating them before they become too serious.

Make sure your kitten gets off to a happy and healthy start

RESEARCH
Studies show that the depositing of facial pheromones has a very calming effect on cats, making them feel safe and secure. You can observe cats doing this naturally when they rub their head from side to the side against furniture, the corners of walls and so on. Scientists have now developed a synthetic version of these facial pheromones, which is available in spray or diffuser form for use in your home, your cat's travel carrier and so on to help reassure him and reduce his stress levels. Some vets use pheromone sprays or diffusers in their surgeries, and can supply these to clients.

Happy birthday!

Everyone loves kittens, and whether they are the result of careful family planning or a happy accident they all deserve a loving home and a good start in life.

Knowing how to care for a pregnant queen (female cat) is vital to ensure her kittens arrive in the world as healthy and content as possible.

Preparation and pregnancy

Before a pedigree queen visits a stud cat for mating, she should be tested for feline immunodeficiency virus (FIV) and feline leukaemia (FeLV) to avoid the transmission of disease.

A cat's pregnancy averages between 63 and 70 days, and apart from obvious weight gain there are other signs to look out for:

- At 21 days the teats will become enlarged and turn a deep pink colour.
- Some queens experience mood changes and become more affectionate than usual during pregnancy.
- The queen's appetite will also increase. To help maintain her strength, her food intake should generally be at least one-and-a-half times what she normally eats, increasing to double when she is nursing her kittens.
- Some queens experience episodes of vomiting during pregnancy – the equivalent of human morning sickness.

RESEARCH

The oldest cat to have kittens was recorded in May 1987, when a 30-year-old called Litty produced two healthy offspring. The average number of kittens in a litter is four, but queens are capable of delivering many more. On 7 August 1970, a legendary brown Burmese named Tarawood Antigone produced one female, fourteen male and four stillborn kittens by Caesarean section.

It is generally best to keep your pregnant cat indoor in a clean, stress-free environment so that you can provide her with all the extra care and attention she needs.

Labour day

As the big day approaches the queen will start to become restless as she searches for a dark, quiet place in which to give birth. Some of the places she might choose (under a wardrobe, for example) can be rather awkward for you to access should assistance be needed. Keeping her in a quiet room and providing her with a comfortable kittening box is probably a safer option. An ordinary cardboard box with an opening cut out of the front for easy access is fine.

Some cats have practice contractions for up to a week before the birth, but once the contractions are five minutes apart – sometimes you can see them happening, and the queen may growl at her stomach – you know the kittens will soon be appearing. Most queens give birth without any help but it is important to determine when the birthing process has finished (see Happy cat tip). Seek veterinary advice if you are at all concerned about the wellbeing of the queen or her kittens. If a queen experiences strong contractions for an hour with no sign of kittens appearing, she may need veterinary assistance. After each kitten is born its afterbirth (placenta) will be expelled and it is important to check that one has been passed for each kitten.

New arrivals

When the kittens are born they will be blind, deaf and totally dependent on their mother. The queen will lick each kitten to remove the protective sac in which he has been born and clear his nose and mouth so that he can breathe properly. The average weight of a newborn kitten is 75–100 g (3–4 oz), and they must be kept warm to survive.

Leave the care of newborn kittens completely to their mother and avoid handling them until they are at least two weeks old.

Happy cat tip

If your cat is pregnant, ask your vet to examine her to estimate how many kittens she is likely to have so that you have an idea of what to expect. A veterinary check-up 24 hours after the birth will also help to ensure that all is well, and that no unborn kittens remain inside.

Neutering

Most responsible owners have no wish to breed from their cat or add to the growing number of cats and kittens in need of good homes. The surgical procedure known as neutering helps to prevent un-wanted pregnancies and curb behaviours such as roaming or fighting, as well as reducing the risk of some feline diseases.

A kitten as young as five months can be sexually mature and capable of breeding. One charity estimates that a single un-neutered female cat is capable of producing 50 million animals in ten years. This figure may sound unbelievable, but is the estimated total number of offspring theoretically produced through future generations if the queen has two females in every litter, with five litters per year.

Sooner not later
Neutered male cats are referred to as castrated, and neutered female cats as spayed. Kittens become sexually mature at about six months old, sometimes younger, and traditionally it has been recommended that cats are neutered between four and five months of age. However, the improved safety of anaesthetics and surgical techniques means that some vets now recommend neutering much earlier, between eight and 12 weeks, with no reported side effects.

There is no evidence to support the myth that a queen will be happier if allowed to have a single litter of kittens, but plenty of evidence to show that un-neutered females that have not had kittens often develop phantom pregnancies and womb infections, and are at risk of breast cancer.

Uneasy life
Living with an un-neutered cat can be unpleasant if you are not prepared for some disruption and inconvenience. Unspayed females come into season every few weeks and will experience agitation, bleeding and frustration, not to mention a very loud and insistent yowl as they call out for a mate. Un-neutered males will roam, become unhappy and aggressive, and may even start mounting other pets or their owner's leg if they don't find a feline friend!

Neutering is a relatively routine procedure, but no surgery is without risk and your vet will discuss this with you beforehand. Thankfully, most cats recover swiftly, and are allowed home on the same day. Female cats may need to return seven to ten days later to have their stitches removed (although some vets use dissolvable sutures), but apart from that you will not be inconvenienced.

RESEARCH

Sexually frustrated un-neutered cats are more likely to stray and research shows that nearly one in every two cats that go missing never return to their owners. Strays that do return are more likely to do so in the first week.

Personality problems

Some people fear that neutering a cat will somehow change his personality. There is no need to worry as there will be no dramatic changes, although many owners report that their cat seems happier and much more relaxed. By monitoring and adjusting his diet you can also ensure he doesn't put on weight – many owners worry that because the cat no longer spends time actively searching for a mate this may lead to weight gain. Your vet will be happy to discuss any concerns you may have, but when considering neutering it is worth noting that neutered cats also have a significantly greater life expectancy than those left entire.

Your cat will be happier and much more relaxed

Common ailments

No matter how well you try and care for your cat, you cannot protect him from every ailment or injury. By nature cats are curious creatures and liable to end up in trouble from time to time!

Happy cat tip

Don't forget to treat your home for fleas, as well as your cat's blankets and bedding. Your veterinary surgery may sell anti-flea preparations for use on carpets, curtains and soft furnishings. Washing your cat's bedding and putting his toys in the freezer for a day or two can also help.

Thankfully, most common problems are not serious provided that you deal with them promptly, and your cat will soon be back to his usual happy self.

Fleas, ticks and worms

All cats are prone to fleas, ticks and internal parasites, but particularly those that love to hunt and have the freedom to roam outdoors. However, contemporary living and central heating mean that fleas are no longer a seasonal problem but an all-year-round nuisance. A flea infestation may cause skin irritation, infections, hair loss and allergic reactions, all of which will result in a very unhappy cat.

Over-the-counter treatments for fleas include collars, sprays, foams and tablets, but spot-on applications (where a drop or two of insecticide is dropped onto the fur of your cat's neck), which are available from your vet, are safe and extremely effective. Some flea products also help to control roundworms, ear mite infestations and ticks.

Worming treatments for roundworms, tapeworms and lungworms are available as granules, tablets, pastes, spot-on applications, injections and oral liquids. For the safest and most effective treatments, consult your vet.

Hairballs

When cats groom themselves, some of the hair is inadvertently swallowed and can become lodged in the animal's gut. If it doesn't pass through the intestines, it may later be vomited up. Most cats get hairballs occasionally but longhaired and semi-longhaired cats are more prone. The first time you observe your cat trying to vomit up these sausage-shaped masses of hair it can be extremely alarming, as his efforts will often be accompanied by violent heaving and strange retching noises.

If you groom your cat regularly to get rid of loose hair you will help to prevent this problem, but some cats seem prone to hairballs no matter how much their owner intervenes. Pet food manufacturers have recently developed new diets designed to overcome the problem and your vet can advise on whether your cat may benefit from one of these. Adding ½ teaspoon of olive oil to your cat's food may help to ease the passage of hair through his system.

RESEARCH

Statistics show that young male cats are more at risk of injury from road traffic accidents than female cats, regardless of whether they are neutered. This may be because male cats tend to be braver than females and are more likely to cross over roads. If you live close to a busy road it may be worth considering whether your cat would be safer living indoors or with restricted access to outside, perhaps by providing him with a cat run (see pages 104–105). Ensuring that your cat is brought safely indoors after dark will also help to protect him, as it is thought that cats may be less able to judge the speed of oncoming traffic at night.

Home and dry

Cats have a reputation for keeping themselves scrupulously clean, and most kittens are housetrained by the time they are ready to go to their new home. However, occasionally soiling problems may occur, which can be upsetting for owners but is generally a sign that the cat is unhappy about something.

Finding the source of your cat's problem is not always easy, but with determination you should be able to work out what is going on and put things right for your pet.

Sudden problems

If your cat has been happily housetrained and suddenly starts soiling in strange places, it is important to check first whether this has been caused by a medical problem such as a urinary infection. Your vet can examine your cat and perform tests to rule this out before you think about how to deal with the problem.

Spraying and marking

A cat with housetraining problems may be using urine or faeces as a marker (see pages 50–51). Indoor urine spraying is usually associated with a characteristic upright stance but can be done when squatting as well, in the same way that your cat uses his litter tray, so it is not always easy to determine what the spraying means. Urine spraying may be a stress response, and is much more common in multi-cat households where an individual's territory can be severely restricted, or he may be bullied or feel threatened.

Clean start

Thoroughly cleaning a stained area is key to discouraging the cat from returning to the same place. Wash the area with a solution of biological detergent and then rinse thoroughly and allow to dry before wiping over with surgical spirits (but do a test on small area of your carpet first in case this affects the dye or fibres). Avoid using detergents containing ammonia, as this is a constituent of urine and may encourage the cat to spray in the same place again.

RESEARCH
Urine spraying is one of the most common problems seen by pet behaviourists. In one study, treatment with a single pheromone diffuser (see pages 72–73) reduced spraying by 70 per cent within multi-cat households.

Kitty litter

In severe cases, your vet may recommend referral to a professional behaviour counsellor. However, before you reach this point consider if anything has changed in your cat's life that may be causing him to feel insecure or unhappy. For example, are you using a different cat litter? If so, change it back again.

Providing a litter tray with a lid, in which many cats feel less vulnerable, and cleaning it out more regularly may help. If you have more than one cat, you will need at least one litter tray per cat, plus one extra so that you always have a clean tray to hand when needed.

Position litter trays in quiet, easily accessible places where the cat is unlikely to be disturbed, and ensure they are not too close to food or water bowls as this could deter him from using them.

Happy cat tip

If your cat has an accident, don't shout at him or grab him by the scruff of the neck as this will make him confused and unhappy, and exacerbate the problem. The calmer you can remain, the greater your chance of resolving it.

The happy mouth cat

One of the most common reasons a cat is taken to the vet is for dental problems. Cats can be very stalwart about enduring discomfort and owners who don't check their cat's mouth regularly are often unaware that there is a problem until the situation deteriorates significantly.

Checking your cat's mouth regularly and cleaning his teeth can help you detect problems early and reduce the risk of him requiring veterinary intervention and anaesthesia.

RESEARCH
There is some evidence that cats fed on dry food have a lower risk of developing dental problems than those fed on wet food. It is thought that the abrasive texture of cat biscuits or kibble helps to prevent the build-up of plaque and tartar. It is also possible to buy 'oral care' diets, which contain lower levels of the minerals that tend to form deposits on the teeth, and are shaped or textured to help clean the cat's teeth as he chews the food.

How do you know there's a problem?

Signs that all is not well with your cat's mouth can include:

• Bad breath (halitosis).
• Difficulty eating.
• Weight loss.
• Taking longer to eat.
• Dropping food from the side of the mouth.

Broken or missing teeth, and/or painful gum disease, can make your cat very unhappy. Check his mouth each time you groom him. Gingivitis (inflammation of the gums) and dental disease caused by the accumulation of tartar (hard deposits made from the minerals in saliva and food), plaque from undigested food and bacteria are the most common problems. Look for inflamed, sore gums and yellow/brown discoloration of the teeth as these may indicate conditions that require veterinary attention.

Cleaning your cat's teeth

The earlier you begin to accustom your kitten to having his mouth handled and teeth cleaned, the more success you are likely to have and the less likely you are to get bitten or scratched (although wearing thin rubber gloves can provide some protection). However, it is probably not essential to clean a kitten's teeth zealously before the age of about six months, as this is when his adult teeth come through.

Always begin when your cat is sitting calmly on your lap. Talk to him quietly and keep your

movements slow and calm so that he remains relaxed throughout. Wrap a piece of gauze around your finger, or put a special tooth-cleaning cap on it (available from pet stores). Gently rub your cat's teeth, and when he accepts this apply a pea-sized amount of special cat toothpaste to your finger and rub his teeth gently. Gradually, perhaps over a few sessions, begin using a cat toothbrush to clean his teeth and improve his oral hygiene.

Some cats appear to be prone to tartar build-up, so don't be disappointed or downhearted if, despite your best efforts, your cat still requires an occasional de-scaling under a light anaesthetic.

Happy cat tip

Always use a specialist cat toothpaste for your cat. Some of these are meat or fish flavoured, which may sound odd to you but your cat will enjoy them! Never be tempted to use human toothpaste on your cat, as it will froth up and taste awful to him, making it highly unlikely that he will co-operate with having his teeth cleaned in the future.

Quick cat checks

Taking time to give your cat a check-up will enable you to pick up on any problems before they develop into something serious. A quick examination will only take five minutes, and if you make it part of your cat's regular grooming session it will soon become part of your routine, which he will accept and you will remember to do!

Happy cat tip

Your cat will not be happy if he has to eat from a dirty food bowl, so dispose of any uneaten food each day and thoroughly wash and rinse his food and water bowls. In addition, remove any soiling from his litter tray at least twice a day. At least once a week, give the litter tray a thorough clean by soaking it in boiling water and disinfectant. Avoid strong-smelling products, as these may put your cat off using the tray.

Some checks can be carried out daily, others weekly or monthly.

Daily checks

- Take time to note your cat's general demeanour and behaviour each day. Always be alert to any sudden changes in his appetite or drinking patterns, any persistent weight loss or obesity, along with any signs of unusual aggression or restlessness.
- Even if your cat is not a longhair, he will benefit from being groomed for a few minutes each day. This will give you the opportunity to check for any obvious problems such as fleas, ticks or scabs, which could mean he has been in a fight and may develop an abscess. If your cat's coat becomes dull and lifeless this too could indicate health problems.
- When your kitten is still very young, get him used to having his gums and mouth checked regularly (see pages 82–83).
- Some pedigree breeds of cat, such as the Persian, are prone to eye problems, so always check for signs of redness or discharge (which could indicate an infection) and bathe them daily (see pages 90–91).

Weekly checks

- Take time to check your cat's eyes (see above) and ears. The ears should be clean and pink although slightly waxy. Evidence of a discharge or foul smell could suggest a bacterial or fungal infection. Persistent scratching of the ears or head shaking plus excess wax may indicate ear mites, which look like cream-coloured miniature spiders or crabs although they are only just visible to the human eye.
- Check your cat's nose and mouth (see pages 82–83), which should also be free of discharge or foul smell.
- Pick up each of your cat's paws and examine the pads to make sure there are no sore areas or pieces of cat litter or gravel embedded in them.

Monthly checks

- Check your calendar to make sure your cat's flea treatments and worming programme (see pages 78–79) are up to date.
- If your cat is on medication, ensure you have enough to last him for the rest of the month, particularly if you are planning to board him or go away for a day or two, leaving him in the care of a neighbour.

6 The pampered puss

Apart from providing your cat with the basics in life, there are a great many things you can do to help make him feel like a pampered puss. Thankfully, most of these ideas don't cost a great deal or take lots of time, but they will undoubtedly make a great difference to your cat's comfort, wellbeing, quality of life and happiness.

However, you need to strike a balance between indulging your cat from time to time, and allowing him to be just that – a cat.

Pampered or over-indulged?

As much as you love your cat and want him to feel pampered and special, it is important to ensure that you allow him to indulge in natural feline behaviours. Making a cat into a baby substitute, or over-indulging him to such an extent that he develops attachment anxiety and frets when you are out of the room, is not a recipe for happiness.

Avoid carrying your cat everywhere and over-protecting him by not allowing him to explore his environment for fear of accidental injury. Cats are incredibly agile and have an innate ability to land on their feet unharmed, even from considerable heights, so try to encourage him to be confident and capable, learning from his own mistakes so that he can look after himself on those occasions when you are not around.

When the cat's away...

At least two Japanese companies are researching and developing clip-on mobile phones for pets' collars, so that owners can talk to their cats when they are apart.

For working owners who are worried that their cat may be bored when they are home alone, help is once more on the way from Japan, in the form of a cat video DVD player. The machine comes complete with a scented remote control smelling of meat and fish, which cats can use to activate a pre-loaded DVD, featuring mice, birdsong and other feline favourites.

Get ready to groom

When it comes to grooming, some cats need more help than others and their needs can change throughout their lives. For example, a senior cat or pregnant queen may have difficulty keeping themselves clean simply because they have become less agile.

This is one area where it is easy for you to make a positive contribution to your cat's happiness.

Why bother?

Cats do like to groom themselves, and if you have more than one cat you may find they enjoy grooming each other occasionally, which is a sign they are bonding happily. However, a thorough grooming with proper brushes and combs helps to remove dirt and dandruff, and stimulates the skin into producing oils that make the coat nice and shiny. Grooming also helps to remove loose hair and reduce the risk of hairballs (see pages 78–79). Cats can become very unhappy if they are not looking pristine, as a matted coat is hot and uncomfortable and lingering odours make them feel vulnerable to predators.

Get kitted out

For you to be able to groom your cat properly, you need to invest in the correct kit. There are so many grooming products available that it is important to know which ones will suit your cat best. Much will depend on the length and type of coat your cat has – if you are in doubt, ask your breeder or vet to advise on which tools would be suitable. Some breeds have woolly undercoats to work through, and longhaired and semi-longhaired cats have thicker coats that require brushes and combs with longer bristles or pins.

A basic grooming kit should include:
- White towel or sheet.
- 2 small bowls for tepid water.
- Cottonwool balls.
- Soft-bristle or slicker brush (with shaped metal pins) for grooming long hair.
- Flea comb.
- Wide-toothed metal comb.
- Round-ended scissors.
- Teeth-cleaning products (see pages 82–83).

In addition, you may like to consider buying eye wipes, coat-conditioner spray, and a grooming mitt or chamois leather to give the coat a gloss. Grooming powder, which acts as a dry shampoo, can help to make combing the coat of a longhaired cat a little easier.

A good experience

If you start grooming your cat from an early age, he should enjoy the experience. However, if for some reason he has developed unpleasant associations with being groomed – perhaps because he has been physically restrained or handled roughly at some stage of his life – you may be able to fool him by investing in a rubber brush with chunky, flexible 'fingers'. As you work over the coat with the brush your cat will feel more as if he is being massaged than groomed. Many cats relax and are much more compliant through this experience.

Grooming your cat

Before you start a grooming
session with your cat, gather all
your kit together. Have some tasty
treats handy to keep your
cat happy and reward
him for being compliant.

Happy cat tip

Spraying some cat coat conditioner on your hands and rubbing them over your cat's coat before you start grooming will help to prevent a build-up of static during the grooming process and make combing the coat easier.

Throughout each grooming session, speak to your cat in a calm, reassuring voice so that he is as relaxed as possible. By taking time to make grooming sessions as pleasant as you can, you will allow positive associations to build and hopefully your cat will run towards you when he sees the grooming kit rather than in the opposite direction!

Watch your cat's body language for signs that he is losing patience with being groomed. Tail swishing, growling, flattened ears and trying to jump off the table are all good clues! Avoid physically restraining him – instead, give him a break for a few minutes before continuing.

Step-by-step grooming

1 Stand your cat on a clean, white towel or sheet to help you detect any flea dirt that may be combed out during grooming.

2 Pick up each of your cat's paws and check them carefully (see pages 84–85). If you find any debris, gently dislodge it.

3 Stroke your cat's head and check inside his ears (see pages 84–85).

4 Using separate bowls of tepid water and a separate cottonwool ball for each eye (to prevent transfer of any infection), gently wipe your cat's eyes, disposing of the cottonwool ball after each wipe. Wipe from the inside of the eye to the outside. Alternatively, use disposable veterinary eye wipes to clean this delicate area.

5 Choose a brush that will help to massage your cat's skin and remove loose hair from his coat (see pages 88–89). You may like to sprinkle unscented talcum or grooming powder on his coat to help remove any grease or stains.

6 Work through the coat with a metal flea comb, looking for little flecks of black flea dirt.

7 Change to a wide-toothed metal comb and gently untangle any matted areas around your cat's ruff, armpits, chest and stomach. If you do find any large tangles that are particularly difficult to comb out, you can cut into them gently with round-tipped safety scissors to help you then tease out the tangles.

8 Finish the session by giving the coat an extra shine with a grooming mitt or chamois leather.

It is also advisable to clean your cat's teeth regularly (see pages 82–83). From time to time it may be necessary for you to trim your cat's claws (see pages 106–107), particularly as he grows older and becomes less mobile, or if he is reluctant to use a scratching post.

Bathing your cat

Unless you are showing your cat, you should not have to bath him often, but if he is particularly dirty, or your vet has prescribed a special shampoo for a skin condition, this may be necessary.

Step-by-step bathing

1 If you are uncertain about your cat's reaction, ask a friend to help with holding him. They can also be on hand to pass you things as you need them, and to help with the rinsing process. Have everything – cat shampoo and conditioner, a soft sponge and perhaps a jug for rinsing – to hand before you start, with some warm, dry towels at the ready so that you do not have to chase a wet, slippery cat around the bathroom if he escapes!

2 Whether you are bathing your cat in the bath or the kitchen sink, put a rubber mat in the bottom so that he has something to grip onto with his claws. This will make him feel more stable and secure, and you will be able to manage him much more easily.

3 Fill the bath with tepid water and then put your cat in. Wet his coat using a sponge or by pouring some water over his body with a jug. Avoid getting water into his eyes or ears.

4 Apply cat shampoo, massaging it into his coat but avoiding his eyes and ears.

5 Rinse thoroughly with tepid water, and if necessary use a second application of shampoo and/or a coat conditioner. A hose attachment on the taps is ideal for rinsing the coat with clean water.

6 When all the shampoo has been rinsed off, lift your cat out of the bath or sink and wrap him securely in a warm, dry towel. Gently towel off any excess water and, if your cat will allow you, use a hair drier on the coolest setting to dry him more quickly.

7 When your cat is dry, use a brush that is appropriate to his coat type to work through the coat, removing any dead hairs and fluffing up the fur to a soft, shiny finish.

8 Give your cat a treat to reward his patience!

Most people assume that cats detest water, but this is certainly not true of all felines. Kittens that have been exposed to water from an early age are more likely to enjoy it and accept having a bath.

Happy cat tip

Always comb your cat thoroughly before you bath him. If you try to comb him afterwards, any tangles in the coat will have dried and 'set', making them much more difficult to remove.

Cautions

Always use cat shampoo on your cat – *never* be tempted to use scented human shampoos. Cats are very sensitive creatures and their bodies are unable to break down many of the chemicals found in everyday products. Shampoos containing high concentrations of tea tree oil can be particularly toxic to cats when they lick their coat afterwards.

Beware of leaving the bathroom door open or bathwater unattended, as your cat may slip into the bath and be unable to get out (see pages 40–41).

Water lovers

It seems that there are some pedigree breeds of cat that really seem to enjoy the sensation of water. For example:

- There is anecdotal evidence that some Abyssinians will actually join their owners in the shower.
- It is a fact that the beautiful Turkish Van loves to swim, and Turkish Angoras and Manx cats also have a reputation for enjoying water.
- In the wild, the Bengali Mach-Bagral cat is sometimes referred to as the 'fishing cat' because of its ability to swim and catch fish using its extra-long claws. Fishing cats are found in parts of India, Nepal, Burma and Southern China.

Kitty kit

Luckily, it is not necessary to spend lots of money in order to keep your cat happy. However, the pampered puss will, of course, have the very best you can afford, and there is certainly plenty of kit from which to choose.

The following is just a small selection from the multitude of items now available.

Collars and tags

The most important thing about a collar is that it must fit properly and come off easily if the cat gets caught on something. If your cat is a hunter, the addition of a bell will help to alert wildlife to his presence. For more information on both these aspects, see pages 48–49.

Identification tags are available in many designs, from plain metal to diamond studded jewels. However, collars and tags can come off, so microchipping is still advisable (see pages 24–25).

Avoid putting a collar on a kitten until he is six months old, as up until then he will be growing fast. When you first put on the collar, choose the lightest you can find, let him sniff it and then stroke him with it so that he realizes it is nothing to be afraid of. Then fasten the collar around his neck, leave it on for a minute and offer tasty food treats to distract your cat before removing it again. Gradually extend the time for which you leave the collar on, until he is happy to wear it continually. Remember to check the collar every few weeks to ensure it still fits properly.

Sleeping beauty

A cardboard box with a warm, soft blanket makes a perfectly adequate cat bed, but there are also some beautiful commercial designs available from pet stores or via the internet. You can choose a basic plastic model or splash out on a feline four-poster, complete with privacy drapes and a faux fur mattress!

Happy cat tip

Why not invest in a couple of comfy bean bags, or the ultimate in feline luxury – a radiator hammock? These are usually made from thick sheepskin or a similar synthetic material that offers the cat some protection from direct contact with the radiator.

Did you know?

The ancient Egyptians were the first to pamper and glamorize the domestic cat. They worshipped the goddess Bast, who had the head of a cat and was the goddess of love and the moon. She was also associated with fertility. When a cat died the entire family went into mourning, and the cat's body was embalmed and placed in a sacred vault.

To help your cat to sleep well, make sure he has washable covers so that they do not become encrusted with dirt and hairs which will be very uncomfortable, and place his bed in a quiet, draught-free corner in a separate area of the room to his litter tray.

Free flow

Every cat needs access to fresh water, but if you really want to indulge yours buy him a pet drinking fountain. Different styles are available, but many cats enjoy those with a free-falling stream of water. Water fountains contain carbon fibres to remove chlorine, odours and debris, which encourages the cat to drink more and helps to improve kidney function.

Dish of the day

There are cat bowls available to suit the interior design of every home, from hand-painted porcelain to gold-plated china. Scratched, chewed or broken bowls can harbour bacteria, so check your cat's bowls regularly and replace them when they begin to look worn. Put water bowls on non-slip placemats so that your cat can drink without chasing his water around the room.

Designer treats

The most pampered cats will enjoy a treat of feline caviar (flaked bonito fish), but it is expensive. Thankfully, most cats appreciate cheaper dried fish-flake treats, available from pet stores and supermarkets.

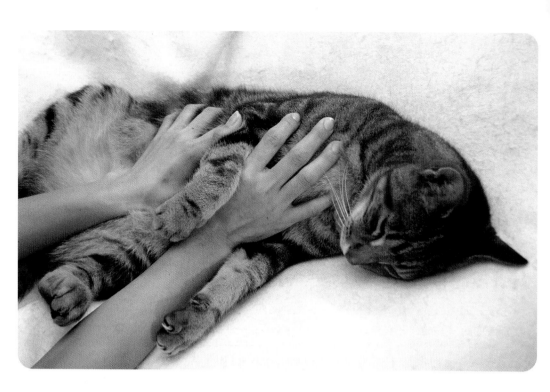

A soothing touch

Most cats adore being stroked and will really appreciate being given a gentle massage. There are many benefits, including helping to ease stiff or aching joints, improve circulation and increase the bond between you.

Giving your cat a massage is easy, fun and, best of all, costs absolutely nothing.

I've had enough!

Some owners find it distressing when a cat that apparently enjoys being stroked suddenly turns round and scratches or bites them. However, it is important not to take this as a sign that the cat dislikes you and instead consider the reason behind it. Some behaviourists think such actions can often be attributed to the degree to which the cat was handled as a kitten and how much tolerance he developed for human contact. Another theory is that prolonged stroking can suddenly make the cat feel vulnerable or remind him of some previous cruelty.

You can encourage your cat to accept stroking by touching only areas that he enjoys, such as his back or the top of his head, and watching his body language so that you stop before he feels threatened. Once he is happy with stroking, you can progress to massage.

> **Did you know?**
> The more your cat enjoys being groomed, massaged and handled, the less worried he will be in a potentially stressful situation, such as when being examined by a vet. You can also ask a friend or other family member to groom your cat and give him a massage so that he realizes being handled is fun.

Healing hands

A cat massage is really just a natural progression from stroking him and is a very easy thing to do, provided that you proceed gently and don't try to manipulate or force the cat's joints in any unnatural way.

1 Massage is best performed when your cat is warm and relaxed so choose an appropriate time, such as when he is sitting outside in a sunny part of the garden or on a warm windowsill. Alternatively, put a heat pack or covered hot water bottle under the blanket in his bed and stroke him gently until he is happy and relaxed.

2 Run your hands down his entire body, from the head to the base of the tail, along the top of the spine and then down both sides. Keep your palms open and the movement fluid, using first one hand and then the other.

3 Use the tips or pads of your first two fingers to apply gentle pressure to his legs, working your way down until you reach his paws. Take his paws in your hands and gently pull them through your fingers.

Happy cat tip

You will be able to tell from your cat's body language whether or not he is enjoying the massage. Some cats will purr in appreciation while others find touch on some areas ticklish and annoying, in which case simply move to another part of the body.

Mini-massage

You can pamper your cat further by giving him a mini-massage and thermal treatment. This will also help to relax him, improve his circulation and ease any joint stiffness. Choose a thick, soft towel and place it on a warm radiator for a few minutes to heat up. Alternatively, spritz it with water and then put it in the drier for ten minutes.

Pick up your cat and gently wrap the warm towel around him, then run each hand over the length of his body from head to tail over the towel. Finish by making small circular movements along his spine.

Flower power

Given the opportunity, most animals will 'self-medicate' if they are feeling ill, and cats are no exception. When outdoors, you will often see them eating grass or other plants, although the reason for this is not always clear.

Happy cat tip
If you are burning essential oils in the home for your own benefit, make sure the room is well ventilated and your cat can get away to a space that is free from the aroma.

However, cats do have difficulty metabolizing the constituents of some remedies, whether they are natural or artificial, and care must be taken when administering aromatherapy products. Man-made remedies such as extracted essential oils, are very powerful and care must be taken to ensure the cat's safety.

Gently does it

Aromatherapy uses highly concentrated essential oils extracted from aromatic plants. The oils in a plant help to protect it from bacteria, viruses, yeasts, moulds and insects. All parts of the plants are used in the extraction process including the leaves, stems, bark, petals and roots, and the resulting essential oils can be highly volatile and up to 100 times more concentrated on extraction than in the plant.

Aromatherapists who are experienced in treating cats recommend the use of hydrolats – by-products of the essential oil production process that are much more dilute and a safer, non-toxic option. You should seek veterinary advice before commencing any aromatherapy with your cat.

Stress-free spritz

If your cat is experiencing a stressful situation such as building work in the home, spritzing the room with a combination of rose, lavender and neroli (orange blossom) hydrolats can be very calming for them.

As hydrolats are so safe, they are also ideal for use as a natural detergent or to freshen soft furnishings and your cat's bedding.

Cautions

Cats are extremely sensitive and it is important never to force them to sniff essential oils or apply them topically, as prolonged use can result in liver damage.

Tea tree oil, which is often viewed as a natural and therefore harmless anti-bacterial substance, can be very potent and toxic to cats if it has not been diluted sufficiently.

Flower remedies

Cats sometimes respond well to the gentle healing powers of flower remedies. Bach Flower Remedies are the originals invented in the 1930s by Dr Edward Bach, who recognized the importance of spiritual and emotional wellbeing and developed 38 'remedies' to help correct imbalances and replace negative emotions with positive ones. There are now many other ranges of flower remedies available, from health food stores and via the internet.

To administer these flower remedies, it is safe to place several drops in your cat's water or some tasty food – but he may well refuse to drink or eat it. In this case, place the remedy on your cat's paws, so that he is encouraged to lick them clean and absorb the remedy that way.

Some owners find that Bach Rescue Remedy, which combines five flower remedies in one, can be very useful if their cat is feeling traumatized by something such as a visit to the vet or cattery.

Living in luxury

If your cat is lucky enough to have a playroom of his own, you can really indulge him by designing and decorating this dedicated space so that he can enjoy hunting, climbing, sleeping and playing. However, most of us don't have the luxury of extra space and are forced to share rooms with our cats.

Did you know?
Vertically striped and textured wallpaper can encourage a cat to scratch, simply because it seems to be a satisfying thing for him to do. Bringing a new piece of furniture into the house, with its novel smell and texture, may make your cat feel a little insecure or anxious, and he may compensate by urine marking. Using a pheromone diffuser can be helpful in this situation (see pages 72–73).

Whatever your circumstances, there is always a lot you can do to create a perfect pad for your cat.

The golden rules

In order for your cat to be happy and content, he will need places that are safe, comfortable for sleeping, and where he can indulge in natural activities such as hunting, hiding and observing.

Interior design tips

• Freestanding, box-shaped units at different heights are very inviting for a cat that is looking for somewhere from which to observe the room. Unfortunately, not all cats are dainty, so store away any expensive or fragile ornaments that may be in danger.
• If your cat has a habit of coming in through the cat flap with dirty paws, place a dirt-attracting mat in front of it to keep floors and carpets clean.
• A tank or bowl of fish will keep your cat amused, but make sure he can't reach inside (see pages 40–41). Alternatively, a lava lamp with free-flowing wax will interest your cat as he watches the changing shapes and movements.
• Indoor cats will enjoy the luxury of an indoor tree to climb, but place large pebbles around the base of the trunk to discourage your cat from using the soil as a litter tray. Alternatively, invest in a tall, freestanding activity centre for him to work off all that excess energy (see pages 54–55).

• Offer your cat a variety of choices of places to sleep. Wicker baskets or a small cardboard box placed on windowsills and filled with a soft blanket or cushion will be very welcome.
• An indoor water feature not only looks great in a home but also helps to provide visual interest for your cat. He will probably sit watching it for hours, and then try to catch the bubbles or fountain flow of water with his paws. This also helps him to improve his eye–paw coordination, making him less clumsy – and perhaps less likely to knock over your favourite ornaments when he leaps up onto a shelf!
• Scratch posts or mats are essential for your cat to feel secure and to be able to sharpen his claws or get rid of broken ones (see pages 106–107).

Perfect planting

Your cat will get a lot of sensory enjoyment from the taste, texture and even the shape of the plants in your garden and home. For example, plants with long, thin leaves will attract your cat to play with them.

As cats are sensitive, some of their reactions can be quite extreme, with certain plants inducing a state of uninhibited euphoria (see pages 46–47). However, not all plants are cat friendly and some are toxic, so take care over which plants you buy.

Friend or foe?

Some plants are poisonous to cats should they decide to eat them, although when provided with a balanced diet and grass to nibble most cats tend to avoid eating other plants that may be harmful. However, it makes sense not to leave bulbs lying around for a curious cat or kitten to investigate. The lists on the opposite page are by no means comprehensive, and your garden centre or vet should be able to advise if you are worried about any of the plants in your garden.

Create a cat jungle

Plant some clumps of bamboo in your garden and watch your cat become king of his very own jungle. Your garden centre can advise on which bamboo will best suit your garden and how big it is likely to grow. Bamboo leaves make amazing shadows and shapes which fascinate cats. They also enjoy wandering through the stems before settling down on the soft, dry leaf matter for a well-deserved siesta.

Cat-friendly plants

Alyssum
Bamboo (e.g. *Phyllostachys*)
Basil (*Ocimum basilicum*)
Begonia
Busy lizzie (*Impatiens*)
Butterfly bush (*Buddleia davidii*)
Catnip (*Nepeta cataria*)
Cat thyme (*Teucrium marum*)
Chamomile (*Matricaria recutita*)
Coriander (*Coriandrum sativum*)
Cosmos (*Cosmos bipinnatus*)

Dahlia
Dill (*Anethum graveolens*)
Forget-me-not (*Myosotis*)
Heliotrope (*Heliotropium*)
Hollyhock (*Alcea rosea*)
Hyssop (*Hyssopus officinalis*)
Lavender (*Lavandula*)
Lettuce (*Lactuca sativa*)
Lovage (*Levisticum officinale*)
Mint (*Mentha*)
Mullein (*Verbascum*)
Pansy (*Viola*)
Parlour palm (*Chamaedorea metallica*)

Parsley (*Petroselinum sativum*)
Pink (*Dianthus*)
Pot marigold (*Calendula officinalis*)
Rosemary (*Rosmarinus officinalis*)
Shasta daisy (*Leucanthemum*)
Snapdragon (*Antirrhinum majus*)
Spearmint (*Mentha spicata*)
Spider plant (*Chlorophytum*)
Sunflower (*Helianthus*)
Tarragon (*Artemisia drancunculus*)
Thyme (*Thymus*)
Umbrella plant (*Schefflera arboricola*)
Violet (*Viola*)

Plants to avoid

Aloe (*Aloe vera*)
Amaryllis
Autumn crocus (*Colchicum autumnale*)
Azalea (*Rhododendron*)
Baby's breath (*Gypsophila*)
Bluebell (*Hyacinthoides non-scripta*)
Burning bush (*Dictamnus*)
Castor oil plant (*Ricinus communis*)
Christmas rose (*Helleborus niger*)
Clematis
Cyclamen
Daffodil (*Narcissus*)
Dragon's blood (*Dracaena*)
Dumb cane (*Diffenbachia*)
Easter lily (*Lilium longiflorum*)
Eucalyptus
Foxglove (*Digitalis*)

Geranium
Ivy (*Hedera*)
Laburnum
Lily-of-the-valley (*Convallaria*)
Morning glory (*Ipomoea*)
Mother-in-law's tongue (*Sansevieria*)
Nightshade (*Solanum*)
Oleander (*Nerium oleander*)
Onion (*Alium cepa*)
Poison ivy (*Rhus toxicodendron*)
Primrose (*Primula*)
Rhubarb (*Rheum*)
Snowdrop (*Galanthus*)
Tiger lily (*Lilium humboldtii*)
Weeping fig (*Ficus benjamina*)
Yew (*Taxus baccata*)

Inside out

A cat run will provide your cat with the opportunity to experience the great outdoors in safety, as well as give you peace of mind in knowing that your pet is not in danger from traffic or other bullying cats.

Even if your cat has free access to the garden, a run can be useful if he is convalescing or you want to restrict where he goes for some reason, perhaps to protect wildlife at certain times (see pages 14–15).

Safety nets

To prevent your cat from climbing over the garden fence and escaping, you can attach netting to angled brackets that are securely fixed to the fence posts, making it virtually impossible for the cat to negotiate. Simple chicken wire or plastic clematis support mesh (available from garden centres) is usually sufficient, and this can be disguised easily with pretty climbing plants. The advantage of barrier netting is that your garden remains virtually unchanged and you and the cat can enjoy it together.

Construction tips

Alternatively, you can purchase a purpose-built cat run or chalet, or commission a carpenter to design and construct one for you. Aim to buy the largest run you can afford, but bear in mind the proportions of your garden so that there is sufficient space available for you both to enjoy.

Before you commit to ordering and paying for a cat run, it is worth checking with your neighbours that they have no objections and making enquiries with your local authority in case planning permission is required. Then shop around, perhaps via the internet, as prices vary considerably. Bear in mind that there may be additional costs such as delivery charges or the price of putting down a solid, level base.

Check to see if your cat run will arrive fully constructed or as a flatpack. Unless you are competent at DIY, consider hiring professional help with some or all of the work.

Creating the perfect den

Outdoor runs are available made from a range of materials including steel and mesh, wood or PVC. Ideally, a run should have prefabricated wired panels around each side, plus a pitched roof for drainage and a secure door with a lock. There should also be a separate, draught-free shelter to which the cat can retreat if he wishes to escape from the heat or cold.

Place ladders, branches and viewing platforms at different heights around the run, so that your cat can get around easily and observe life from a variety of vantage points.

Pots of shade-loving evergreen plants add extra interest and shade, but check that they are not toxic to cats. Alternatively, consider lifting one or two paving stones or drilling holes in a concrete base and planting these with shrubs and other plants that your cat will enjoy. For more information on specific plants, see pages 102–103.

Your cat run should contain a clean litter tray and a supply of fresh water. Then provide lots of hidden treats and toys to make sure the time your cat spends in his outdoor 'den' – up to a maximum of about three hours a day – is especially happy and enjoyable.

Claw care

Your cat needs his claws to help him balance, defend himself and catch prey, and to provide visual and scent signals that help to reassure him.

When your cat digs his claws into his scratch post, leans back and pulls, he is exercising and toning his upper body. A scratching cat is a happy cat!

Say 'No' to de-clawing

The practice of de-clawing is illegal in most parts of Europe but still common in the USA and Canada. De-clawing is not just a radical manicure, it is the amputation of the last bone of each toe. In human terms, it is the equivalent of

chopping off the ends of each finger. The procedure is so painful that it is used to test the effects of strong analgesia.

Many de-clawed cats develop behaviour problems such as refusing to dig cat litter and toileting in inappropriate places. To make your cat happy, leave him with his claws intact and provide him with ample opportunity to use them.

Cover up

A recent innovation is the use of covers that slip onto a cat's claws to prevent him scratching. Welfare charities advise that these can make a cat feel vulnerable and unable to defend himself and should only be applied by experts as a last resort, possibly as a short-term solution to a behaviour problem while the underlying cause is investigated and resolved.

Up to scratch

Scratching is a normal and essential element of feline behaviour. It is done to help remove the outer sheath of the claw, which helps to sharpen the claws, and releases pheromones that help to make the cat feel happy and relaxed.

Every cat needs access to one or more scratching posts. You can also get scratch mats which lie flat on the floor, and some cats enjoy using these. The earlier you introduce your kitten or cat to a scratch post, the less likely he is to scratch your furniture. Rubbing the post with dried catnip will encourage him to investigate it and soon he will be digging his claws in with delight. Position the post where your cat likes to spend time, such as by a sunny windowsill or close to his bed, as most cats like to stretch and scratch when they wake up from a nap.

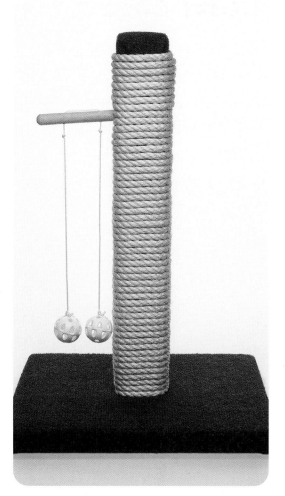

Happy cat tip

Once you have put your cat's scratch post into position, try not to move it too much. Your cat will scent the post and may feel insecure if it is suddenly relocated.

Make your own

A tree branch or wooden log can make a perfect scratch post and, of course, costs nothing. Alternatively, you can make one easily by securing a heavy post to a sturdy base. The scratch post must be taller than the cat at full stretch and must feel very stable and secure, as if it falls over he may refuse to use it again.

Cover the post with different textures to see which one your cat likes best: try winding rope around it, or covering it with carpet on one side and sisal on the other. Some cats like scratching on cardboard – these scratching posts are available to buy, but you can also make your own from corrugated cardboard or the inner tube of a carpet roll.

7 Feline fun

There is nothing more fun for a cat and owner to enjoy than a good game. However, while this may be simple entertainment and pleasure for us, for cats it has a more important role to play by helping to stimulate and satisfy some of their basic instincts.

Finding toys and games that can tap into your cat's natural urges to stalk, chase, pounce, catch, bat and bite will please him most.

All the right moves

Playing helps to develop a cat's social and finer motor skills, plus eye–paw coordination. A single kitten will need lots of interactive play with his owner to help satisfy his developing hunting instincts. After he has been weaned a kitten's games change into predatory play, and this is when you first notice those 'mouse pounces', 'bird swats' and 'fish scoops'. All of these moves can be encouraged with a variety of games involving chasing, throwing and the kitten balancing on a perch. Allowing your kitten to chew the object after he has 'captured his prey' brings some completion to the task and is something he will find very satisfying.

Adult cats can be less demanding, particularly if they have access to a garden, as they can usually find plenty of natural stimuli to satiate their hunting needs. However, it is still advisable to play with an adult cat at least once a day, so that he regards the home as another place where he can enjoy fun and games.

Breeds apart

Some breeds of cat seem to expect and demand, their owners to play with them more than others.

Oriental breeds such as the Siamese and Burmese have a reputation for being full of energy, which if left undirected can sometimes become destructive. Scheduling regular play sessions can help to keep these cats entertained and out of trouble.

In contrast, the British Blue or some of the longhaired breeds, such as the Persian or Ragdoll, will be content with less energetic play, but still enjoy the attention of their owner when it is offered to them. Some of these more placid breeds don't always instigate play, but it is important to try to motivate them as this can help to increase your cat's mobility and combat obesity.

During play, take into account your cat's age and health, and adapt games as necessary by making them shorter or less strenuous so that he does not incur any injuries (see pages 150–151).

Toy time

Pet stores and supermarkets
stock a wide range of toys and
games that have been developed
specifically for the entertainment
of your cat. Gone are the days
when he had to make do with
playing with a ball of wool.

Happy cat tip

To keep playtime happy, remember the
golden rule: rough play signals the end of
play. Your cat will soon realize that he must
play gently for the fun to continue.

Today's manufacturers have spent a fortune
designing toys that will help to keep your cat
happy by exercising his natural behaviours.

Which toys?

Visit any retail centre and you will see shelves full of brightly coloured, non-toxic cat toys. It is fun to buy a selection and see which ones amuse or motivate your cat the most.

You will find toys your cat can hunt, stalk and 'capture', as well as toys for him to retrieve and bring back to you (see pages 114–115). There are also puzzle toys, where food treats are hidden inside a toy or box with holes in it through which your cat puts his paw and tries to get the food out. These are excellent for improving eye–paw coordination and mobility, and some cats really enjoy the motivation of this as a daily challenge.

Interactive toys, where the owner operates part of the toy to make it bounce, dance or roll along the ground to encourage the cat to try to catch it, are excellent for helping to increase the cat–owner bond.

Playtime rules

- Store your cat's toys in a special box with a lid and give them to him in rotation to maintain his interest in them.
- Inspect your cat's toys from time to time to ensure there are no rough edges or broken pieces that could injure him or might be swallowed.
- Keep toys on elastic or string strictly for supervised play sessions, to avoid the risk of

your cat getting himself tangled up and accidentally strangled.
- It is better to have several short play sessions of a few minutes each during the day, rather than one long session of an hour or so that culminates in the cat becoming tired or bored.

Extra fun

Some cats like toys that squeak, but avoid any that are too loud and don't squeak them too close to his ear, as this could frighten him.

You can buy tubes of bubble mixture that have been scented with things cats like, such as catnip. Have fun floating a trail of bubbles for him to chase and see his expression when one pops before his eyes!

Toys to make

As with children, the toys that cats like best are often the simplest and most inexpensive of all. They frequently prefer to play with the cardboard box or other packaging in which the toy or game was wrapped!

RESEARCH
Studies show that kittens start playing with objects and each other from about three weeks old. Interestingly, females in litters of mixed sexes tend to play more with objects than those in litters comprised solely of female kittens.

You don't have to spend a fortune on cat toys, and with a little imagination you can provide your pet with a range of playtime fun.

Bags and boxes

Cats love to investigate things, and climbing into a cardboard box or large paper bag will interest the ever-curious feline. Once he is inside, try scratching the outside and watch him 'attack' the mysterious intruder.

Paper

Birthdays and holiday festivals are not only exciting times for people. Trailing brightly coloured wrapping paper along the floor can help to stimulate your cat's chase instinct and he will relish the sensation of sinking his claws into it. You can also add to his enjoyment by providing him with paper of different textures, and rolling some up into balls of different sizes for him to bat along the floor and play with.

King of the castle

Save some strong cardboard boxes of different sizes and glue them together to make a play area for your cat to explore. Cut holes in the sides and through the top, some small enough for just a paw to pop through, others large enough for the entire cat to jump inside. Throw a few favourite treats into the 'castle' and then watch as your cat leaps in to find them.

String and feathers

Cats are fascinated by string, especially when it is being trailed along the floor. Try attaching objects to the end, such as coloured ribbon or some feathers, to increase the allure.

Table tennis balls

Cats love playing with these little balls, as they are so light and mobile. If you watch a kitten play with a table tennis ball, you will see him approach it somewhat tentatively at first before giving it a tiny pat. As the ball rolls away, the kitten thinks of this as an invitation to chase it, and quickly learns to 'dribble' like a football player. These movements are exactly the same as he would make if pursuing and trying to control a mouse.

Cotton reels

If you enjoy sewing, or know someone who does, you can collect cotton reels to make toys for your cat. Thread them together on varied lengths of string for him to chase, or simply roll them towards him so that he can practise his dribbling skills.

Fishing rod

You can make fishing rod games easily, from a thin branch or length of dowel. Simply tie feathers or a small, lightweight toy to the end on elastic or string, but avoid real fishing line as it could damage your cat's gums. Your cat will enjoy leaping to catch his 'prey' as you move the fishing rod around.

Caution

Never allow your cat to play with plastic bags, as he may become entangled in the handles and risk suffocation.

Games to play

The kinds of games you can enjoy with your cat are really limited only by your imagination, and the more effort you put into trying to engage with him, interact and have fun, the better the quality of your time together will be.

Some cats prefer one type of game to another, so if yours doesn't seem particularly interested don't be disheartened – simply think of a new game and start again.

Time to play

Your cat may well have what is sometimes referred to as a 'mad half hour' at a particular time each evening, perhaps due to a build-up of energy and a simple need to let off steam (see pages 16–17). Scheduling a play session for this time can help to direct your cat's energy in a positive way, and you can end with a quieter game and a cuddle to help settle him down for the night.

Catch the mouse

There are many toy mice available on the market, with some even remote controlled and designed to mimic the erratic movement a mouse might make when chased. However, a simple soft toy either thrown or attached to a piece of string is an easy and inexpensive way of instigating this type of hunting game. If you are worried that the mouse has eyes or ears which might come off and be swallowed, remove them beforehand – your cat won't mind at all!

Don't forget to allow the cat to win the game from time to time, or he will eventually become disheartened. When he has caught the 'prey', allow him to mouth it, throwing it up in the air and catching it, in the same way that he would a real mouse.

Fetch

Some breeds of cat seem almost dog-like in their behaviour and are very willing to retrieve toys. Oriental breeds such as the Siamese often seem to enjoy this, but some crossbreeds enjoy playing fetch too.

To find out if your cat will fetch, choose a small, lightweight toy in which he has shown an interest. Call the cat's name and when he is looking at you throw the toy up into the air several times, catching it yourself. If your cat comes over to investigate, try throwing the toy a short distance and then wait to see if he fetches it back for you. Offer lots of verbal praise if he does and then throw the toy again. Remember that not all cats will retrieve, and if after a number of attempts your cat seems disinterested, simply find another game to play.

Once your cat has got the idea of fetching, you can make the game more difficult for him by throwing the toy out of sight – perhaps behind a chair – so that he has to find it before bringing it back. It is always better to finish a game before your cat gets bored, so practise for only five or ten minutes at a time.

Acrobatic cats

Young, agile kittens and cats are never happier than when they are climbing, exploring, stretching and jumping. These activities offer both mental and physical stimulation and will help to keep them fit.

You can encourage your cat to have fun by developing games on different levels and providing opportunities for as much athleticism and mobility as possible.

No ambush

Although it may seem fun to allow your kitten to hide behind the sofa and ambush your feet, it will not be such a good idea when he is fully grown so you should not encourage this when he is young.

Find some tasty treats and lay a treasure trail around the room

Discourage games that involve your cat pouncing on your fingers and toes, such as moving them underneath a blanket or tapping them along the side of a chair so that he jumps up and tries to catch them, often with sharp, extended claws. Restrict these types of games to some of the toys in his toy box and he will soon get the message.

Treasure hunt

Find some tasty treats and lay a trail around the room for your cat to find. Start off with one or two and gradually make the treasure hunt more difficult, hiding a treat underneath an empty yoghurt pot or on a shelf that he has to jump onto. Do make sure your cat eventually finds, and eats, all the treats, or you may wonder why there is a strange smell in your house some days later – before discovering a prawn that has fallen down behind a radiator!

Obstacle race

Enlist the help of any children in your family and construct a little obstacle course for your cat to negotiate. Useful items include boxes, ladders, hoops and cardboard inner tubes. Encourage your cat to race through the course by luring him with treats or a toy.

Happy cat tip

Young, cute kittens often get lots of extra attention and playtime from their owners, but sadly the time spent playing with them often drops significantly when they become adult cats. Remember: to keep your adult cat healthy and happy he will still need interactive games and to spend fun, quality time with you each day.

Tunnel time

If your cat enjoys playing inside a crinkly paper bag, he may well enjoy going inside a crinkly cat play tunnel. You can buy these made specifically for cats, but a child's play tunnel is just as good, although it may take up more room in your house. Luckily, most tunnels fold down flat when not in use and are easy to store away. Threading a toy through the tunnel on a piece of string or throwing treats inside will help to encourage your cat to investigate it.

Up and down

Tie a toy to a string or piece of elastic then sit at the top of your stairs and allow it to drop down several steps. Your cat will run down after it and you can gradually pull it back up again, occasionally allowing him to catch his 'prey'.

Actvity centres

Cats love to play and climb on any type of activity centre, and there is a wide range of designs available from pet stores or via the internet. For more details on activity centres, see pages 54–55.

Training your cat

All domestic cats are capable of being trained to a certain extent, first by their mothers and then by their owners. Coming when called, using a litter tray and allowing themselves to be groomed, for example, are all forms of training and co-operation with their owners.

With patience some cats can be trained to quite sophisticated levels, although they will only allow you to do so if they think it is worth their while!

Clicker training

This type of training is sometimes referred to as operant conditioning, using a clicker is a relatively new but highly successful training method. The trainer uses a small, lightweight plastic box that makes a clicking noise when a button is pressed. Many different types of clicker are available, but basically the training works by identifying a behaviour you would like from your cat, such as to come when he is called or to sit, and then immediately clicking and rewarding him for complying with a high-value treat such as a tasty prawn or a favourite toy. Quite quickly the cat will associate the clicking noise and the treat with that particular behaviour, which you then mark with a verbal command such as 'come' or 'here'.

Practise with the clicker before you introduce it to your cat

Practice makes perfect

The key to successful clicker training is your ability to operate the clicker accurately. It is vital that you click at exactly the same time as the animal performs correctly, in order to get him to repeat that behaviour in the future. If you imagine the clicker as a tiny camera, which you press when you want to record a photo of something, you will realize that clicking a second too early or too late means you are clicking for something completely different, such as the cat walking away from you.

Practise with the clicker before you introduce it to your cat. Try throwing a ball up into the air or against a wall and timing your click for the exact moment the ball hits the ground.

Schedule training sessions for a time when your cat is feeling a little hungry: just before mealtimes is ideal. Keep the session short, and finish with something the cat enjoys.

Have some small pieces of chicken or cheesy treats to offer as rewards. Throw one or two down so that he knows you have them, and the next time you offer one simultaneously use the clicker in order to associate the two. Don't use the clicker too close to his head as the noise may frighten him.

Target training

To get your cat to nudge an object such as a pencil or wooden spoon on command, try rubbing the end of the 'target' stick with something tasty. As soon as the cat's nose touches the target, click and give him a treat. Repeat this several times, until the cat realizes what you want him to do. At this point you can mark the behaviour with a verbal command such as 'touch'. Eventually, you will be able to walk around the room with the cat following your hand or the target stick, using just the verbal command and occasionally rewarding with a food treat.

Happy cat tip

Never physically punish a cat, and avoid shouting as this will make him anxious and confused. If your cat doesn't behave in the way you want him to, increase the value of the treats you are offering when he does get it right and reward more frequently.

Out and about

As you get to know your cat and enjoy his company, you may decide he has special qualities that you would like to share with other people. Perhaps he is exceptionally friendly, stunningly beautiful or extremely agile.

Today there are many opportunities to show your cat, do voluntary work or even compete with him. However, you should only pursue activities your cat seems happy to do.

Therapy cat

The health benefits of pet ownership are scientifically proven. Research also shows that many patients in hospitals, residential homes and hospices enjoy seeing and petting cats, which is an

activity that helps to relieve stress and boredom and ease symptoms of depression.

If you have a very placid cat that enjoys attention from different people, he may be suitable for use as a therapy cat. Although dogs are the most common therapy animals, a small number of cats are also used for this purpose. The cats undergo personality assessments and health checks before being given the all-clear to accompany their owners on voluntary visits.

If you are interested in finding out more about therapy cats, search for appropriate charities on the internet or enquire at your local library.

Show time

If you have a show-quality cat or kitten and are meticulous about grooming, you can get a lot of fun from showing him. This can be an interesting and sociable pastime, provided you don't take it too seriously and can accept disappointment with good grace. Show-quality kittens are the best the breeder has to sell and therefore the most expensive. They must be registered with the appropriate show sponsor organization.

Even though you may have a show-standard kitten, judges are also looking for those that are extrovert, easily handled and that enjoy being shown. If your cat appears to dislike the entire experience, then he may not have the temperament for showing and pursuing this activity will make him unhappy.

> ### Happy cat tip
> If your cat is not lucky enough to win a rosette at the show, don't blame him in any way or let him feel your disappointment. Simply pick him up, give him a cuddle and reassure him that in your eyes he will always be a winner!

There are also show classes for non-pedigree cats, and fun classes such as cat with the longest whiskers or best markings, so visit some shows and find out what is available in your area.

Agility

If your cat shows prowess at climbing, jumping and negotiating obstacles, then he may be suited to the new sport of cat agility. This fledgling sport is taking off in the USA, where it is wowing the public as cats demonstrate their natural athleticism and grace. Competitions are scored as the cats follow lures through hoops and tunnels, and active non-pedigree cats perform just as well as pedigrees. Major cat associations and feline nutrition companies are beginning to take note of this new sport, which encourages the cat–owner bond, and it is expected that cat agility will soon make its way into Europe.

Quality time

The more time you spend with your cat, the happier he will be and the more your relationship will be strengthened. It can be very calming just to sit quietly with your cat, and stroking him will help to lower your blood pressure and relieve stress.

While your cat will enjoy playtime, grooming and being out and about with you, he will also be extremely happy simply to sit down and enjoy some special time together.

Social work

Whether you have acquired a very young kitten or an adult cat, he will benefit from an ongoing course of socialization to help him adapt and adjust to his new environment. Your breeder or rescue centre should have already embarked on this, but you can help by introducing a few new sounds and situations each day, so that the bond between you increases and your cat learns to cope with different scenarios.

Here are some ideas to include in your socialization programme:

- Invite one or two new people to handle the cat each day, and offer him a treat. Include children, older people, someone in uniform and/or wearing glasses, carrying a walking stick, and so on.
- Accustom the cat to seeing an umbrella being put up and down.
- Ring your mobile phone near him, using different ring tones.
- Turn on the radio and television at different volumes. If possible, play a sound-effects CD of fireworks or a thunderstorm from time to time (see pages 130–131).

- Accustom the cat to getting in and out of his carrier (see pages 126–127).
- Take him on short car journeys.
- Lift the cat onto a table and run your hands over him as a vet would.
- Examine his teeth, gums and ears regularly (see pages 82–85).
- Take the cat out into the garden and explore it together.
- Ring doorbells and ask people to walk in and out of the room past the cat, sometimes stopping to pet him, other times just walking past.
- If your neighbour has a friendly dog, gradually introduce your cat to him – ask for the dog to be kept on a lead during this process.

Gradual changes

Although cats like routine (see pages 42–43), it is unrealistic to expect that there will never be times when this is disrupted.

If you know there is going to be a major change to your cat's routine, such as a new baby or pet arriving, plan ahead so that he can begin to adjust. For example, allow your cat to smell a blanket the new pet has used before the animal arrives, so that this becomes familiar to him.

8 Vets, pets and scary stuff

As much as we all want to make every day a happy one for our cats, there will obviously be some that are better than others.

Sometimes things happen that the cat perceives as unpleasant, such as visiting a cattery or builders starting work in the home, but if he is prepared as much as possible for these events the stress will be reduced and he will cope much more happily.

How cats show distress

If your cat is suffering from stress, whether from a real or a perceived threat, he obviously cannot verbalize the way he is feeling. As his owner, you may have to turn detective to determine what is troubling him.

In the early stages you may notice that your cat is increasing activities that he finds reassuring, such as becoming exceptionally clingy towards you or repeatedly rubbing the furniture to mark it with pheromones (see pages 72–73). Fortunately, pheromones are odourless to humans and we are therefore unaffected by them. Unfortunately, this is not always the case with other markers, such as urine or faeces, and if your cat demonstrates toileting problems this may well be a response to stress (see pages 80–81).

Other signs of distress include listlessness, loss of appetite, refusal to go out, sleeping more than usual, or a tendency to illness as the immune system struggles to cope.

Coping mechanisms

It is not always easy to uncover the causes of a cat's unhappiness, but asking yourself when a problem began and what changes were occurring at that time may help to provide clues. Socializing your cat as much as possible will help him to adjust and cope with different situations (see pages 122–123), as will being determined not to allow him to become over-attached to you, no matter how much you adore him (see pages 30–31). Some cats can become distressed by even a brief absence from their owner, which makes enforced absence – through vacation, for example – a very traumatic experience. Encourage your cat to accept and enjoy the company of other people, so that he can cope better in a cattery or if a neighbour has to look after him.

Happy vet visits

While all vets are qualified to care for cats, some specialize in their treatment or have a natural affinity for them. Personal recommendation is probably the best way to find a cat-friendly vet.

It is in everyone's interests for a cat's visit to the vet to be as stress free as possible, as it makes the job of examination and treatment much easier. The more homework you undertake to help prepare your cat for his vet visit, the happier he will be.

Stay cool for cats

When you take your cat to the vet, put his favourite blanket and some of his toys in the carrier with him plus a few of his favourite treats (unless your vet has specifically asked for him not to be fed), and offer him one or two during the consultation. You may also find that spraying his carrier with pheromone spray (see pages 72–73) helps him to feel a bit more settled and secure.

To keep your cat calm, speak reassuringly but try to act as normal. If you seem anxious, or act differently by cuddling him more than usual, your cat will begin to wonder if there is something he should be worried about and behave accordingly.

Carry cat

If your cat has only unpleasant associations with his travel carrier, it is no wonder that he hides as soon as you fetch it from the cupboard. If you then have to start searching for him, or persuading him to come out from his hiding place, you may be in danger of being late for your appointment and getting more stressed by the minute, thereby exacerbating the whole problem.

The key to a stress-free vet visit is to arrive calmly, with your cat as happy as he possibly can be. To do this, he must enjoy going into his carrier. So, don't hide the carrier away in a cupboard, but ensure your cat sees it every day so that it is just another piece of furniture. Leave it out near his bed or activity centre, with the doors open and a particularly cosy blanket inside.

To encourage your cat to investigate the carrier of his own accord, put a few tasty treats inside or incorporate the carrier into one of his games so that he has to go inside to retrieve a toy. Once the cat is inside, spend a minute or two talking to him and stroking his head. If you can begin to build positive associations with the carrier, your cat will regard it as his den and enjoy going inside.

Dummy runs

Practise taking your cat on short car journeys – make sure the carrier is securely strapped into the seat so that it won't fall off during an emergency stop. Most veterinary surgeries are happy to arrange for cat owners to call in and see them during a quiet time so that they can say hello, take the cat out of the carrier and give him a treat. Your cat will then build positive associations with the smells and sounds of the surgery. In addition, accustom your cat to being handled and examined at home, so that he is happy to accept this from the vet at his next visit.

The key to a stress-free vet visit is to arrive calmly

Happy holidays

There will inevitably be occasions when it is necessary for you to board your cat at a cattery, or find someone to care for him while you are away on vacation.

Knowing your cat is content and well cared for during your absence will give you great peace of mind, and will allow you to enjoy your holiday to the full or concentrate on the work you have to do.

Choosing a cattery

If you have cat-loving friends, ask them to recommend a cattery, or check out the advertisements in your veterinary surgery, telephone directory or local newspaper. Entrusting the care of your precious cat to a stranger should not be undertaken lightly, so visit the premises and meet the proprietor to make sure the facilities are of a good standard.

A cattery should be licensed with the local authority and the certificate should be clearly displayed in the reception area. The proprietor should be happy to meet you and answer your questions, as well as asking you lots of questions about your cat such as his age, name, breed, medical history and whether he has any special requirements.

When you view the cattery, check that it is clean and tidy, and if there are dogs there that they are kept well away from the cat area. Each cat chalet should have a separate sleeping area and exercise run, and contain a scratch post, clean litter tray, bed and bedding, heat lamp, and a shelf for

resting and sunbathing. There should be a sufficient gap between the chalets to protect the cats from airborne diseases.

Scaredy cats

Being physically removed from home, with all its familiar territorial markings, can be traumatic for a cat, particularly if he has a timid or shy personality. The use of a pheromone diffuser (see pages 72–73) in the home can help to reassure him that all is well on his return.

Pet sitters

While some cats appear oblivious to changes in their surroundings, others find this more difficult to cope with. If your cat is one of these, then employing a professional pet sitter or asking a cat-loving neighbour to help out may be a more humane solution than boarding him at a cattery. A pet sitter can live in your home while you are away or call in twice a day to feed your cat, play with him and clean out his litter tray. Leaving the radio on and ensuring your cat's toys are rotated (see pages 54–55) will help to keep him occupied between visits.

Contact details

Whether you leave your cat in a cattery or in the care of a neighbour or pet sitter, make sure you provide contact details in case of an emergency. Include your phone numbers, the name and phone number of your vet, insurance details, and the phone number of a friend who can be contacted in an emergency to authorize treatments if you are not available.

Happy cat tip

Take your cat's bedding and a few of his favourite toys to the cattery with him, so that he is surrounded by reassuringly familiar smells. If you have more than one cat and they get on well, they may find it stressful to be separated from each other so arrange for them to be boarded together.

Fright night

Some cats are more sensitive than others, and the slightest hint of a thunderstorm or firework will send them running for cover. Others are more placid and seem unperturbed by any disturbances life throws at them.

RESEARCH
Studies show that anti-anxiety medication can be useful in the short term for treating fearful cats, but a combination of noise desensitization and pheromone diffusers is the most effective long-term strategy.

Thankfully, there is a lot you can do to help a scaredy cat become a courageous cat.

Bangs in the night

Celebrations commonly feature fireworks as part of the festivities, and many cats find these absolutely terrifying. If you know that a firework party has been planned in your neighbourhood and your cat is likely to be severely traumatized, you could discuss this with your vet, who may have practical suggestions to help keep your cat calm and, in severe cases, may prescribe anti-anxiety medications.

Don't panic!

A cat can easily panic and run away if suddenly startled by a loud noise or flash of lightning, so make sure yours is wearing a name tag on his collar and is microchipped (see pages 24–25). During the firework season, make sure your cat is safely indoors as soon as night begins to fall. Keep the curtains closed, turn up the volume on your television or radio to help drown out the noise, and provide him with a litter tray even if he doesn't normally have one so that he doesn't have to venture outside.

Your cat will pick up on your own anxiety, so to keep him happy it is important for you to stay calm and act normally. Although it is a natural reaction to comfort your cat if he is scared, behaviourists believe this can exacerbate the problem because it confirms to the cat that there is something of which to be afraid. If your cat hides behind the sofa during a storm, it is better to ignore him than to pull him out and give him a cuddle. If he sees you sitting quietly, he will be much more likely to come out of his own accord.

CD therapy

If you have played your kitten a firework or thunderstorm CD as part of his socialization programme, he may already be accustomed to the noise and cope more easily. However, it's never too late to start a desensitization programme with your cat – the CDs are available from veterinary surgeries or via the internet. Play the CD at a very low volume when your cat is doing something enjoyable such as playing or eating his favourite food. Gradually, over a period of days and weeks, play the CD more frequently and at louder volumes, until the cat hardly notices the noise at all.

First-night nerves

If you have followed the tips on pages 40–41, your home will already be cat-proof and well prepared for your new pet's arrival. However, the first few days and nights in a new home can be stressful for him.

Taking steps to ensure this settling-in period is as peaceful and enjoyable as possible will help to give your new cat confidence, enabling him to cope more quickly and become a much-loved family member.

Home aroma

A few days before you pick up your kitten or cat, visit the breeder, owner or rescue centre and take a blanket or old jumper with you to be placed in his basket. When you collect your cat, bring the blanket home with you and the smell of it will remind him of home and be very comforting.

Family life

Children will undoubtedly be very excited at the prospect of a new cat. However, it is important to explain that the cat may quickly become overwhelmed if they are too loud or boisterous around him. Ask them to handle him gently and quietly (see pages 44–45), and give him lots of opportunity to sleep and recover from the move.

Home time

When you arrive home with your cat, double check that all the doors and windows are closed before you open his carrier.

Allocate a room for the cat to live in for the first few days or weeks. This is where you should put his bed, litter tray, toys, scratch post, food and water. There should also be one or two places for him to climb up on or hide behind if he feels a little anxious. The kitchen is usually one of the busiest rooms in the house and may not be ideal for the cat's first days, particularly as there are so many places in which he could hide or get lost.

Over the next few days, as your cat settles down you can gradually allow him to explore different rooms in the house, but shut him away at night in 'his' room.

On the first night, play a game with your cat, pop him on his litter tray and then put him on your knee so that you can gently stroke him until his eyes close and he starts to fall asleep. When this happens you can lift him onto his bed, continue to stroke him for a few minutes and then leave him to sleep. A well-covered hotwater bottle, plus his comfort blanket, will help to keep him happy.

Of course, if you want your cat to sleep in your bedroom that is up to you, but be prepared for him to wake early and expect you to play with him!

Happy cat tip

If you have another pet, be careful not to rush the introductions. For advice on introducing other animals to your cat, see pages 134–135.

Socializing

During the first days and weeks, gradually introduce as many people as possible to the cat, asking them to handle, stroke and generally make a fuss of him so that he realizes people are friendly and forms positive associations (see pages 122–123).

Meet the dog

If your new kitten or cat is from a home with a cat-friendly dog, he is much more likely to tolerate canine attention. However, if he has had a bad experience you will have problems persuading him that not all dogs are scary.

> **Did you know?**
> Cats trot by moving the two legs on one side and then the two legs on the other. Dogs, like most other mammals, move their legs in diagonal pairs. Cats share their unusual gait with camels and giraffes, although there is no obvious connection to help explain this. This method uses the least amount of energy and helps to ensure speed, agility and silence, perfect for when a cat is hunting.

If you already have a dog or are thinking of getting one, you will need to do your homework first or you will have a very unhappy cat on your hands.

Breeds apart

Some breeds of dog are more tolerant of cats than others, although there are exceptions to every rule. Dogs can be dangerous to cats and may even kill them, so err on the side of caution, particularly with a dog of unknown breeding or background.

- Hounds and terriers that have been bred to hunt in packs and kill their prey are high risk for cats.
- Given the opportunity, herding dogs such as Collies will often try to round up a cat, although it is sometimes possible to train the dog to override this instinct.
- Retrievers may try to pick up a kitten and carry it around, and while they do have soft mouths this may not be appreciated.
- Care should be taken with dogs bred for pursuit behaviour. All dogs have a chase instinct that is triggered by fast, sudden movement and a scared, fleeing cat can be too much of an invitation to resist. Racing dogs such as Greyhounds are not necessarily more likely to chase a cat than other breeds, but they are more likely to catch him!
- Dogs bred as companion animals are often best suited to living with cats. Labradors and Golden Retrievers have a good reputation as family pets and often tolerate cats very well.

Pleased to meet you

You should introduce cats to other pets, including dogs, very gradually. The more time you take, the better. During those early days, when the kitten lives in a separate room, his smell will pervade the rest of the house and alert other animals to his presence. By gently wiping a cloth over the cat's face and putting it in the dog's bed with some treats on top, you can begin to develop positive associations before they even meet.

For the first meeting, keep the cat in a carrier or indoor crate and the dog on a lead, intervening as little as possible if there is initial hissing and spitting and rewarding calm behaviour with stroking and verbal praise. Avoid shouting or physical punishment at all costs, as this will reinforce a negative association.

Repeat the introductions until the cat and dog seem tolerant of each other, then put the dog in the crate and allow the cat to roam around. Never leave a cat and dog together unsupervised until you are certain they are friendly with each other.

Fight night

It can be very distressing when two cats that normally live together quite happily suddenly develop an inexplicable fear or loathing of each other. Uncovering the reason behind this is not always easy.

However, you will need to find out what is going on if you are to restore harmony to your home.

Irretrievable breakdown?

Unfortunately, even at the best of times the relationship between cats in a multi-cat household can be tenuous and suddenly break down, particularly if they are kept indoors.

It is thought that indoor cats are more likely to develop fear aggression than outdoor cats, simply because they are less able to escape from what they perceive to be threatening or stressful. For example, one cat may start sitting in front of a cat flap or doorway to prevent another cat using it. This could intimidate a less dominant cat, which may then develop behaviour patterns the owner finds problematic, such as toileting in places other than the litter tray. Behaviourists report that feline toileting problems are the most common reason owners seek help with their cats.

RESEARCH
Studies show that cats in a multi-cat household, and particularly those that are sedentary, overweight and middle-aged, are more likely to develop urinary tract disease than other cats.

Happy cat tip
If your cats develop a relationship problem, seek early professional help. Consult your vet and, if necessary, consider referral to a behaviour counsellor. Many insurance policies will cover the cost of this.

Good neighbours

In general, oriental cats such as Burmese and Siamese may try to dominate a more placid breed such as a British Blue or a Persian. It is generally a good idea to avoid putting cats with extremes of character together (see pages 32–33).

In severe cases of hostility, it may be necessary to separate the cats completely and then reintroduce them gradually. However, this is best done with the help of a professional behaviour counsellor (see Happy cat tip).

Limited resources

If you have not changed anything in the home by, say, bringing in a new pet, then something may have happened to the cats to which you are oblivious. It could be that a new cat in the area has come up to the window or even entered the house through the cat flap. Magnetized cat flaps can help to stop intruders but may not restore confidence once this has been eroded.

Make sure your cats have adequate resources and access to them at all times (see pages 56–57). You need to be certain that no one cat can dominate or guard a particular area, depriving another cat access to it. In addition, ensure you give each cat equal attention from you.

In a multi-cat household, the cat that controls the best perches on shelves, activity centres and so on is generally the most dominant. The highest cat is literally the 'top cat', and those on the floor are subordinate. In a fearful situation, a cat's ability to retreat to a high observation point helps to reduce stress.

Stay calm

Shouting at a cat does not resolve problems and could actually make them worse, particularly in the case of attention-seeking behaviour. Stay calm and try distraction techniques to defuse the situation, such as rattling a box of biscuits or trying to initiate play.

On the move

Cats are territorial creatures and the familiar sounds, sights and scents of home all help to make them feel secure and content. Travelling or moving to a new home can be quite traumatic for some cats, and being in a strange environment can make them feel vulnerable and unhappy.

Not all cats are severely affected by moving to a new area. Indeed, some very placid types take it in their stride and enjoy accompanying their owners on vacation. Generally speaking, however, most cats prefer the comforts of home and, provided arrangements are made for their care, would rather be there than anywhere else in the world.

Happy moving day

If you are relocating to a new home, you can either book your cat into a cattery for a few days while you pack up your belongings and move, or arrange for a neighbour to care for him. The third option, particularly if you are moving some distance, is to take the cat with you. However, this will require some forward planning. If your cat is very nervous, it may be advisable to seek veterinary advice and, if necessary, administer anti-anxiety medication to help keep him calm and relaxed.

Travel tips

Some days before you move, allocate a room for your cat to stay in (preferably one with which he is already familiar) and put his bed, scratch post, litter tray, food bowls and so on in there so that he feels secure and happy with all his things around him. On the day of the move, make sure the cat is locked into this room and that the removal men do not have access to it, until you are ready to put the cat into his carrier and take him to his new home.

Happy cat tip

Remember to update your cat's microchip database with details of your new address and telephone number. Give these details to your neighbours too, just in case your cat returns to his old home at some future date.

Otherwise he may run off, which would be very inconvenient as well as extremely upsetting.

If you are travelling some distance, ensure the cat has access to water throughout the journey and does not become overheated or stressed.

When you get to your new home, allocate your cat a quiet room once again so that you can put his bed, litter tray, food and so on in there, and lock him in while the removal men unload your furniture. The familiar smells of his bed, blanket and scratch post will help to reduce the stress of moving to a new home. Keep your cat in this room for a few days, until he seems to be confident and is eating and behaving normally.

How long you wait before you allow your cat to go outside will depend on your cat's personality, but vets recommend four weeks to allow him to adjust to his new surroundings. Schedule his first outing for just before you feed him, so that he is likely to come back for his meal. Accompany your cat outside and encourage him to walk around the garden with you, but allow him to dictate the pace and if he doesn't want to explore then simply accept that he will do so when he is ready. Don't be tempted to carry your cat around, as this will not allow him to scent mark the area and find his way back next time.

Schedule his first outing for just before you feed him, so that he is likely to come back for his meal

Wild at heart

Feral cats may seem unloved and unhappy, but if this is the only life they have ever known then being forced to endure the attentions of people or cooped up indoors would be impossible for them.

However, with a patient approach and good management techniques, it is possible to make a feral cat happier.

What are feral cats?

Feral cats are the offspring of wild cats, or stray and un-neutered abandoned cats. They live in small groups or colonies and are distrustful of people, having never been socialized to them. They will not allow themselves to be approached or touched.

Some welfare groups advocate a trap, neuter, return (TNR) policy for feral cats as being the most humane way of controlling the population. The cats are trapped, taken to a veterinary surgery and neutered, vaccinated, then the tip of an ear is surgically removed as a visible sign that they are no longer entire and the cats are then returned to their colony to live out the rest of their lives.

Homing a feral cat

If a 'wild' cat has had some experience of people in the past, perhaps before he became a stray, it is sometimes possible for him to overcome his fear and accept the touch of a human hand, and ultimately be rehomed.

Taking on a feral cat is not something to be done lightly, and care should be taken to ensure that this is not just a cat that wanders from house to house and is cared for by several people. Cat charities are always looking for homes for feral cats, and some are ideal for living in a barn or on a farm to help keep down vermin, as an environmentally friendly form of pest control. If you live in a rural area and have appropriate facilities, it may be worth contacting them for further information. Pest-control cats still require regular food, water, shelter and veterinary attention in order for them to lead happy lives.

Feral kittens that are found before the age of six weeks are usually quite easy to tame, but it is important that they are tested for blood

diseases before they are allowed to live in a home with another cat.

If you find a feral cat, kitten or even a whole litter, contact an animal welfare society that can offer advice and, if necessary, arrange for the animal to be seen by a vet and scanned for a microchip (see pages 24–25).

Taming with treats

Time, patience and a willingness to accept setbacks and disappointment are the keys to dealing with feral cats.

Placing a tasty treat, such as prawn or a piece of chicken, on the end of a pole may eventually encourage the cat to take it. Throwing treats out to the cat and gradually moving them in nearer will begin to build positive associations with humans. Taking food from your hand is a major step forward, but even then the cat may not accept being stroked.

Caution

Feral cats are often very afraid, so do take care when attempting to deal with them. Sturdy gloves are an essential piece of kit to protect your hands.

9 Keeping an older cat happy

Once your cat reaches the age of ten years he is considered to be a senior or geriatric, although you may not notice any obvious physical changes or problems for several years. Provided you take care of your old-age pet, feed him well and keep him mobile, he can continue to be happy and well for many years to come.

Improved veterinary medicine, feline nutrition and the education of owners have all contributed to the increased longevity of domestic cats. Today, more cats are neutered than ever before, and this has undoubtedly led to fewer cats straying and being killed on the roads or suffering injury or disease (through being bitten or scratched by an infected cat) by fighting.

The ageing process is not a disease, and your cat will still enjoy being played with, cuddled and provided with a variety of toys. As he grows older, you may have to adapt the games and make them shorter, but gentle exercise will help to keep him mobile and physically stimulated.

Feline dementia

Scientists have now confirmed that geriatric cats can develop a feline form of Alzheimer's disease. Symptoms of feline dementia include loss of memory, disorientation and behaviour problems.

Recent studies suggest that 28 per cent of pet cats aged 11–14 years are likely to develop at least one age-related behaviour problem and this increases to more than 50 per cent for cats over the age of 15. The good news is that with environmental changes, veterinary treatment and occasionally ongoing medication, it is possible for some of these behaviour problems to be rectified and managed.

Experts suggest that a combination of good diet, mental stimulation and companionship can reduce the risk of dementia in both people and cats. If owners and their cats live in a poor environment with little company or stimulation, the risk of dementia increases. However, if an owner plays with their cat regularly, and provides them both with a diet enriched with antioxidants, this will help to ward off dementia (see pages 150–151).

The nine lives of a cat

It is not easy to equate a cat's age directly to human years, because the ageing process is faster in the early stages of kittenhood and then slows down considerably in adult cats.

Happy cat tip

If your older cat used to be the most dominant in a multi-cat household, he may gradually find himself usurped by a younger housemate. Keeping a close eye on the situation is essential to ensure the older cat is not deprived of food, water or litter trays.

As with humans, every cat tends to age differently: some ten-year-old cats are still very kitten-like while others are happy to doze their days away peacefully.

How old?

Generally speaking, at the age of one year a cat is probably the equivalent of a 15-year-old teenager. After that, things tend to slow down somewhat and one adult year is considered equal to about four human years, so that an 11-year-old cat is similar physiologically to a 55-year-old person. Cats tend to live longer than dogs and the average age is now 14–20 years, with indoor cats living the longest. The world's oldest recorded cat was 36 years of age, but this is exceptional.

Physiological changes

The first thing an owner usually notices is that their cat is beginning to slow down, sleeps more and generally takes things easier. Cats will naturally always sleep much more than dogs and conserve their energy, but they tend to do this even more as they grow older.

Some cats develop painful joint problems such as arthritis and medication can significantly increase their mobility and quality of life. Muscle tone also reduces, which again contributes to an older cat being less agile and mobile.

Lack of mobility or painful joint disease means that your older cat may have more difficulty keeping himself clean and well groomed, and will need extra help from you. In addition, reaching up to use the scratch post effectively may be problematic, so you should examine his claws regularly and have them clipped as necessary.

Metabolism and appetite can change as a cat ages, with some eating more and others less (see pages 150–151).

Sometimes an older cat will appear to undergo a personality change, becoming calmer than in his youth or sometimes more grumpy. Luckily, it is much more common for a cat to become even more affectionate and loving in old age than he was as an extrovert, lively kitten. However, any dramatic changes in personality should always be investigated by a vet to rule out a physical cause.

An outdoor cat may decide he now prefers the indoor life, and providing a litter tray will be necessary and appreciated.

RESEARCH

Because cats are living longer, veterinary surgeons are seeing more illnesses related to old age – such as dementia or arthritis – than in the past. Owners are more willing to try to help their cats live happy, healthy lives than ever before, and scientists are working on many research projects to help develop new drug therapies to combat the effects of the ageing process.

Coping with a disabled cat

Some cats are born with disabilities, such as deafness or blindness, while others develop them through injury or illness in old age. In fact, cats can cope remarkably well with varying degrees of disability.

Happy cat tip
While it is tempting to be over-protective towards a disabled cat, it is important to allow him as much independence as possible in order for him to be happy.

Nevertheless, there is no doubt that the support and encouragement of their owner is invaluable in helping such cats get the most out of life.

Loss of a limb

If a cat has to have one or more limbs amputated it is very upsetting for the owner, but not necessarily completely catastrophic. Cats have an amazing sense of balance, and while walking, running, jumping, climbing and pouncing will all undoubtedly be affected, they usually find a way to adapt.

It is important to liaise with your vet on a regular basis and assess your cat's quality of life, particularly if there is paralysis and incontinence to consider. In some cases, a specially designed mobility cart may help to provide some independence again. These carts were initially developed for dogs but are now available for cats as well. They work by supporting the cat's hindquarters and tail so that they don't drag along the ground. Success depends on the cat's age, personality and degree of disability, but many owners are thrilled with the results.

At home, it is important that you encourage your cat to be as mobile as possible, perhaps by moving furniture closer together to enable him to step from one to another more easily. Providing ramps up to chairs on which you are happy for your cat to sit can also help. As he grows in confidence it may be possible to rearrange the furniture back into its normal position.

Blindness

A cat with limited or no vision is vulnerable, particularly outdoors where there is traffic, so supervised trips to the garden are essential. Blind cats rely on familiar smells to find their way

around, so in the house keep furniture in the same positions and rooms clear of clutter. Treasure trails of treats can encourage mobility.

Your blind cat will enjoy playing with noisy toys, such as those with bells or a squeak. Scrunched-up paper that makes a sound when he bats it with his paw can be a great source of fun.

Avoid carrying your blind cat around too much as this will disorient him, and always put him down somewhere he is familiar with such as next to his food bowl, bed or litter tray.

Deafness

An older cat may experience hearing loss, and the first sign you may notice is that he ignores you when you enter a room. Always ask a vet to check out physical causes for behaviours such as this.

A deaf cat is vulnerable to traffic and won't be able to hear such things as barking dogs, so make sure he is kept indoors or safely supervised when he is out in the garden.

Fitting your cat with a collar with a bell will help you to locate him, as he obviously won't come when you call him.

RESEARCH

In June 2003, German acoustics expert Hans-Rainer Kurz announced the invention of a feline hearing aid. It had taken two years to develop with help from experts at the University of Veterinary Medicine in Hanover. While not a cure for deafness, this aid enables the cat to take the usual acoustic signals and rework them into sounds in the brain.

Make your old cat happy

As your beloved cat enters his senior years, there is a great deal you can do to help him enjoy this special time in his life.

Making some simple changes to your routine and adapting your home in small ways can make a huge difference to his comfort and quality of life.

Happy cat tip

Don't be tempted to think that getting a curious little kitten will be just the thing to perk up your older cat. Older cats resent change and will not appreciate the attentions of a young kitten. Keeping your cat's routine as regular as possible and giving him plenty of loving attention are the two things that will keep him happy in old age.

Sleep matters

As with older people, a senior cat will tend to sleep more and be less active than he once was. The ageing process can result in lack of muscle tone and a thinner coat, providing him with less body warmth. For this reason it is important to keep an older cat warm, perhaps by moving his bed closer to the radiator or fire and maybe providing him with several radiator hammocks, although he may need help getting in and out of them as he grows older. Bean bags are ideal as extra beds around the home, as they help to support old bones and are very stable.

Many cats are allowed to sleep on their owner's bed at night, but if yours is not you should remember that the temperature can fall quite dramatically once the heating is switched off at night. Giving him extra blankets, a fleece or even a covered hotwater bottle or heated pad in his bed will all help to provide extra warmth and comfort throughout the night.

Cats are not always careful about how close they get to a fire when they are seeking a warm place to sleep, and singed whiskers are commonplace. If you have an open fire, make sure a fire guard is in place (see pages 40–41).

Indoor, outdoor

An older cat that feels the cold can often seem reluctant to go outside, particularly on a cold and rainy night, so providing him with an indoor litter tray can help to prevent toileting problems. If your cat does go outside and comes back in wet and cold from the rain, towel him down gently with a warm towel before popping him into his bed to dry off completely.

If your cat is outdoors during the day when you are at work, make sure he has access to a warm, dry shelter.

Older cats with arthritic joints can sometimes have difficulty going through a cat flap, so tying it open can help them.

A helping hand

As your cat ages and stiffens up, you may need to put a small stool or stack of cushions near his favourite windowsill so that he can continue to climb up on to it to sunbathe. Warmth from the sun seems to be particularly beneficial in helping to ease a cat's aches and pains, but keep an eye on him if he likes to sleep in a hot conservatory for any length of time as he could suffer from sunburn or become overheated.

Exercise and nutrition

While your older cat may be happy to doze his days away, it is important that you try to keep him as mobile as possible.

Helping him to exercise gently and managing his diet so that he eats and drinks properly will ensure he retains his inner kitten for as long as possible.

Happy cat tip
Laying a treasure trail of favourite food treats can be a great way of encouraging your cat to mooch around a room during the day when you are out at work.

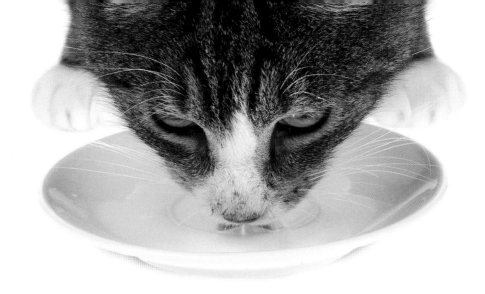

Keep on moving

Your older cat may seem reluctant to go outside as much as he did in his youth, but encouraging him to explore the garden on a warm day will help to keep him mobile and alert. If you are going outside to do a spot of gardening or even just to sit with a drink and a book on a warm summer's evening, take your cat with you. The change of scenery and new scents and sounds will all help to stimulate and entertain him.

Try to engage your cat in some gentle play sessions, perhaps by dragging a twig or some leaves on the ground to interest him. Avoid energetic games where he has to jump up to try to catch something you are waving in the air, as this can be painful for old joints.

In the home, use your imagination to help your cat retain his interest in games, taking into account his age and medical history. Make games shorter and less exuberant to avoid the risk of injury.

RESEARCH

Studies show that increased levels of omega-3 oils in the diet can help to keep your cat's joints free, supple and mobile, and to maintain a healthy heart and circulation. Ask your vet's opinion on feeding supplements to help improve your cat's mobility.

Feeding the older cat

Pet food manufacturers have developed a range of high-fat senior foods designed to help keep older cats in good condition. Many of these are rich in antioxidants and the amino acid L-carnitine, which have been shown to be beneficial to older cats by boosting the immune system and maintaining condition, so you may like to consider feeding one of these diets.

Healthy older cats tend to drink less than they did when younger, and it may be worth changing your cat's food to one with a higher water content to help compensate. You can do this by changing from dry to wet food, or adding a gravy to dry food. (Always introduce any dietary changes very gradually, to avoid gastric upset, and consult your vet first.) Place more water bowls around the house for your older cat to encourage him to drink as much as possible.

Consider investing in a set of food and water bowls on stands so that your older cat doesn't have to bend down so far to eat and drink. Ensure they are at the right height for him, though, as reaching up could cause him pain.

If your cat has teeth missing or other dental problems that make it difficult for him to eat dry food, pour on a little hot water to soften it and make a palatable gravy. Ensuring food is at room temperature or has been heated for a few seconds in the microwave will help to tempt a finicky eater.

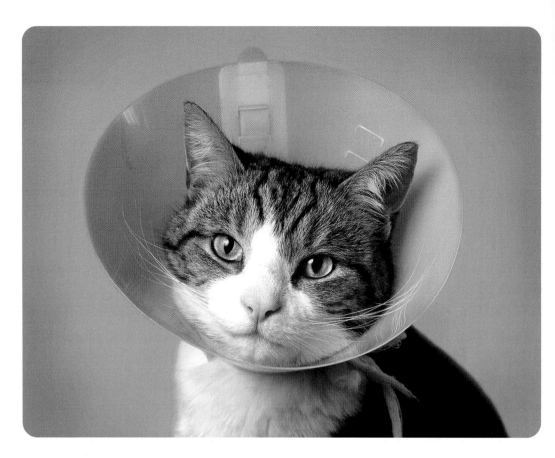

Vets, meds and the older cat

Geriatric cat medicine has improved dramatically over the past few years and undoubtedly contributed to the increased longevity of the domestic cat.

Taking advantage of new developments and being proactive about your older cat's health will help you to keep him in tip-top condition.

Senior health clinics

Once your cat reaches his senior years, the ageing process accelerates and it is advisable to increase the regularity of his annual check-up to twice a year. Many veterinary surgeries run clinics for geriatric cats at which they are weighed, blood tested and examined to try to identify and treat problems early. Older cats can be prone to the following health problems:

• Arthritis.
• Loss of hearing or vision.
• Diabetes.
• Kidney disease.
• Thyroid malfunction.
• Urinary tract disease.
• Liver failure.
• Heart disease.
• Tumours.
• Senile dementia.

Weight issues

Some cats have a tendency to put on weight during old age, others become finicky eaters and have difficulty keeping weight on (see pages 150–151). Your vet will check your cat's weight and advise you accordingly, but weighing him between visits will help you monitor the situation.

Prescription diets

If your cat is diagnosed with a health problem such as kidney disease, your vet may prescribe a special diet for him. Such diets are generally only available from your vet and have been proved to aid greatly in the treatment of long-term or chronic health problems.

Vaccines

As cats grow older, some owners wonder if it is necessary to continue with annual vaccinations. Some vets agree that sufficient immunity to disease will have built up over the years, while others recommend continuing with boosters as the older cat's immune system becomes less efficient with age, making him more vulnerable to disease. You should discuss the subject of vaccinations with your vet before making an informed choice.

Caution

Cats are unable to metabolize many substances and a number of common human medications can be potentially life threatening to them. Never give your cat medicines such as aspirin or paracetamol, and always seek medical advice before administering drugs that have not been prescribed by a qualified vet.

Complementary therapies

As well as conventional veterinary medicine, some owners like to experiment with holistic medicines to improve their cat's health and wellbeing. Some qualified vets also practice holistic medicines such as acupunture, homoeopathy and herbalism, but unfortunately there are also many unqualified alternative medical practitioners who claim to be able to help animals but in fact have no scientific knowledge and can cause a great deal of harm. Always seek the advice of your vet before embarking on any alternative therapy for your cat, and make sure the practitioner you choose is qualified and registered with the relevant professional body.

Never give your cat human medication such as aspirin or paracetamol

Happy endings

No matter how well cared for your cat may be, there will ultimately come a time at the end of his life when you have to say goodbye.

Every owner wishes that this will happen naturally, but it can also be very comforting to know that you provided your cat with the best quality of life and – as a final act love – a humane and peaceful death.

Euthanasia

Euthanasia is the term used when a vet injects an overdose of strong anaesthetic that will stop the functioning of the cat's heart and lungs. It is a quick and painless procedure, and one that vets carry out regularly, although this doesn't mean they find it an easy thing to do. Many vets build up a close relationship with clients and their cats, but are nevertheless professional enough to do their job without becoming emotional.

If your cat has been ill for a long time, or is in

Many surgeries provide pet bereavement counselling

chronic pain with little or no quality of life, your vet may suggest euthanasia as a more humane option than invasive or non-helpful treatments. Often the impact of a cat's illness on the owner plays a part in the decision: it can be an emotional and financial burden to care for an elderly, sick cat that is incontinent and in constant pain.

Discuss everything with your vet beforehand, sign the necessary consent forms, and arrange to have a friend or family member with you at the time. Decide beforehand what you want to happen to the body, so that you can leave the surgery immediately and begin the grieving process.

Guilt and relief

Some owners are able to remain with their cat during euthanasia, while others fear becoming too upset and causing distress to the cat. Veterinary nurses are very experienced at taking over in these situations and understand completely how traumatic this can be.

Occasionally you may feel relief immediately afterwards, particularly if life has been particularly hard for both of you for some months. This, too, is a normal reaction and not one to feel guilty about.

Coping and moving on

Everyone deals with grief differently, but research identifies several stages to be worked through. These include anticipated loss when you know the inevitable is coming, shock and denial immediately afterwards, emotional pain and eventually recovery.

It is important to talk through how you are feeling, but be careful who you speak to as the last thing you need is someone telling you to 'Pull yourself together, it was only a cat'. Many surgeries provide pet bereavement counselling, and some charities also offer this service via either telephone or email.

Happy memories

There are many ways to help recall the happy times you shared with your cat. Children, who are often more stalwart at dealing with death than adults, may like to talk about their cat, draw pictures of him, write stories and poems and so on. Adults can put together a photograph album, create a scrapbook, commission a painting or tapestry, plant a rose bush or set an engraved plaque in their cat's favourite part of the garden, or just create a quiet area in which to reflect on days gone by.

New beginnings

Not experiencing the warm welcome
of a cat when you come home can
seem a huge gap in your life, but it
may take some time before you feel
ready to acquire another.

Once the initial grief at losing your cat has worn
off and you are able to recall your old friend with a
smile rather than sadness, it is probably time to
consider opening your doors and your heart to a
new feline friend.

Keeping other cats happy

There is some evidence that cats can suffer from
grief if they lose a feline companion to whom
they were particularly close. Symptoms can
include sleep disruption, where the cat sleeps
either more or less than he did before; moping and
vocalization, where the cat wanders around
yowling as he searches for his friend; lack of
appetite, or comfort eating; and general clinginess
towards his owner.

Although it is natural for an owner to want to
comfort an existing cat, particularly if they too are
grieving and understand the pain of loss, it is not
always useful to prolong this. If you can act as
normally as possible, keep to the cat's routine and
encourage him to play and have fun, you will find
that he returns to his old self much more quickly.

A cat that had always been subordinate to the
one that died, may actually come out of his shell
and flourish, once he realizes he is now top cat in
the house and can go where he likes without fear
of a feline reprimand.

Cat companions

If you have always kept two cats and decide to get
another as a companion for your existing one,
take care to introduce them properly (see pages
134–135). The smells and markers of your previous
cat will remain in the house for some months to
come, so it is important to do everything you can
to help the new cat settle in with as little stress as
possible (see pages 132–133).